THE UNIFORM RESIDENTIAL APPRAISAL REPORT HANDBOOK

Compiled and Edited by
THE NATIONAL ASSOCIATION OF
REAL ESTATE APPRAISERS

Published by
TODD PUBLISHING, P.O. BOX 5837, SCOTTSDALE AZ. 85261

$15.00

Published in the United States of America by Todd Publishing, Scottsdale, Arizona 85261.

First Printing, 1988

Copyright © 1988 by the National Association of Real Estate Appraisers. All rights reserved. No part of this publication may be reproduced; stored in a retrieval system; or transmitted in any form or means, electronic, mechanical, photocopy, recording or otherwise, without the prior written consent of the publisher.

Library of Congress Catalog Number: 88-50320

International Standard Book Number: 0-935988-33-5

The statements or opinions appearing in this textbook do not necessarily reflect the view point of the National Association of Real Estate Appraisers or its individual members.

* Note: The guideline references are subject to change. Revisions and updates occur from time to time. Therefore It is recommended that the appraiser keep abreast of the current requirements.

THE UNIFORM RESIDENTIAL APPRAISAL REPORT HANDBOOK

TABLE OF CONTENTS

I	PREFACE	
II	THE UNIFORM RESIDENTIAL APPRAISAL REPORT-INTRODUCTION	1
III	THE APPRAISAL REPORT FORM & THE APPRAISAL PROCESS	3
IV	PAGE ONE OF THE UNIFORM RESIDENTIAL APPRAISAL REPORT FORM	5

    A. Subject
    B. Neighborhood
    C. Site
    D. Improvements & Interiors

V	PAGE TWO OF THE UNIFORM RESIDENTIAL APPRAISAL REPORT FORM	23

    E. Cost Approach
    F. Sales Comparison Analysis
    G. Reconciliation

VI	DOCUMENTATION IN SUPPORT OF THE UNIFORM RESIDENTIAL APPRAISAL	39
VII	UNIFORM RESIDENTIAL APPRAISAL REPORT—CASE STUDY WITH ATTACHMENTS	41
VIII	SUPPLEMENTS	47

    A. The Most Common Errors & Deficiencies in Appraisal Reports (A study compiled by the National Association of Review Appraisers & Mortgage Underwriters)

    B. Common Appraisal Deficiencies Identified by Federal Housing Authority

    C. Samples of Unacceptable Appraisal Practices—Fannie Mae

    Guidelines References
        Federal National Mortgage Association
        Federal Home Loan Mortgage Corporation
        Federal Housing Authority
        Veteran's Administration
        Farmers Home Administration
        National Association of Review Appraisers & Mortgage Underwriters

PREFACE

The introduction of the Uniform Residential Appraisal Report Form and the growing need for standardization in the Residential Appraisal process has necessitated the need to develop a guidebook to assist the Residential Appraiser in preparing a professional report that would be both consistent and accurate.

This book, developed by the National Association of Real Estate Appraisers, presents a line by line analysis of the **UNIFORM RESIDENTIAL APPRAISAL REPORT**, cross-referenced to Fannie Mae, Freddie Mac, HUD, VA, and the Farmers Home Administration guidelines.

The National Association of Real Estate Appriasers would like to express its thanks to the National Association of Review Appraisers and Mortgage Underwriters for supplying extensive data on the preparation of The Uniform Residential Appraisal Report Handbook.

II   INTRODUCTION

In 1986, the Uniform Residential Appraisal Report Form was introduced by the Federal National Mortgage Association and the Federal Home Loan Mortgage Corporation. The format was adopted for use by these agencies and has also become a standard form for the Veteran's Administration, Federal Housing Administration and Farmers Home Administration.

The Uniform Residential Appraisal Report Form requires more information than it's predecessors, and is intended to provide consistency in appraisal reporting and a more accurate estimate of value. The form was revised to include the most current appraisal methodology and to incorporate the latest changes that have occurred in the appraisal profession.

When the form is properly completed, it should give both the users of residential appraisals and the purchasers of residential mortgages, a clearer picture of the appraiser's analysis and value conclusion.

III THE APPRAISAL PROCESS

Definition of the Assignment

Identification of Real Property
Property Rights Identified
Effective Date of the Appraisal
Assumptions and Limiting Conditions

Preliminary Survey—Data Collection and Analysis

Establish the Identity
Demand and Supply Factors
Data Requirements
Data Sources
Time Element
Estimation of Appraisals Cost

General Data

Economic
Locational
Social
Environmental

Specific Data

Comparative Properties (cost, sales, rentals, ect.)
Property Data (title, site, improvements, ect.)

Highest and Best Use

Approach to Value

Cost Approach
Income Approach
Market Approach

Reconciliation of Value and Final Estimates of Value

Uniform Residential Appraisal Report

IV PAGE ONE OF THE UNIFORM RESIDENTIAL APPRAISAL REPORT FORM

6　The Uniform Residential Appraisal Report Handbook

A. SUBJECT SECTION

The first section of the Uniform Residential Appraisal Report is used to identify the subject property, to describe the property rights to be appraised, and to summarize financing data and sales concessions. The appraiser should complete the subject section of the report initializing information supplied by the client as well as from data contained in the appraiser's own reference materials. Information should be verified by reviewing public records such as tax records, plots of survey and other recognized real estate records and source books.

Property Address			Census Tract	②	LENDER DISCRETIONARY USE	
City	County	State	Zip Code		Sale Price	$
Legal Description ①					Date	
Owner/Occupant			Map Reference		Mortgage Amount	$
Sale Price $	Date of Sale		PROPERTY RIGHTS APPRAISED		Mortgage Type	
Loan charges/concessions to be paid by seller $			☐ Fee Simple		Discount Points and Other Concessions	
R.E. Taxes $	Tax Year	HOA $/Mo.	☐ Leasehold		Paid by Seller	$
Lender/Client			☐ Condominium (HUD/VA)			
			☐ De Minimis PUD		Source	

PROPERTY ADDRESS & LEGAL DESCRIPTION

1. The Appraiser must identify the subject property by its complete property address and legal description; a post office box number is not acceptable. The address should be consistent with the address used on the sales contract and any other legal documents.

CENSUS TRACT

2. Enter the census tract numbers. If property is not in a census tract enter "N/A". Census tract maps may be obtained by contacting the Superintendent of Documents, U.S. Government Printing Office, Washington D.C. 20402.

PROPERTY RIGHTS APPRAISED
☐ Fee Simple ③
☐ Leasehold
☐ Condominium (HUD/VA)
☐ De Minimis PUD

PROPERTY RIGHTS APPRAISED

3. The appraiser must determine the property rights to be appraised "fee simple" or "lease hold".
    • Fee Simple interest is the normal transferable right of property ownership.
    • Lease-hold interest is the right to use and occupy real property by virtue of a lease agreement.
   In addition, the appraiser must indicate whether the subject property is located in a PUD, De Minimus PUD, condominium, or cooperative project.
    • Condominium (HUD/VA) indicate if the interest is held subject to a condominium agreement.

   * **(NOTE: Fannie Mae and Freddie Mac does not accept the URAR Form for condominiums, cooperatives, or PUDs)**

* (NOTE: HUD and VA have approved the URAR FORMS used for appraising Condominiums, Cooperatives, or PUDs)

- De Minimus PUD is fee simple ownership with a partial interest in nearby property, with a small interest or responsibility for the maintenance of common areas. (pool, tennis courts, etc.)

GUIDELINE REFERENCES

> **Fannie Mae - January 1988 - Section 403 - Property Rights Appraised**
>
> The Appraisal for units in PUD, Condominiums or Cooperative projects must be completed on a Appraisal Report - individual Condominium or PUD Unit (Form 1073).
>
> **VA - February 1987 - Paragraph 6a - Property Rights Appraised**
>
> Since VA will utilize this form for all PUD (Planned Unit Development) types, the word "De Minimus" should be deleted in all instances. The required reporting of assessment fees (condominium or PUD) shall be made in the "Comments" block of the Site section.

```
LENDER DISCRETIONARY USE        (4)
Sale Price              $
Date
Mortgage Amount         $
Mortgage Type
Discount Points and Other Concessions
Paid by Seller          $

Source
```

LENDER DISCRETIONARY USE

4. It is the appraiser's responsibility to complete the form in its entirety **except** for the box titled "Lender Discretionary Use". The purpose of this box is to encourage lenders to provide closing dates to comparable sales reporting services.

B. NEIGHBORHOOD SECTION

The neighborhood section of the appraisal report should be complete and accurate. The purpose of a neighborhood analysis is to identify the area - based on common characteristics or trends - that are subject to the same influences as the subject property. The sales prices of comparable properties in the identified area should reflect the positive and negative influences of the neighborhood. Information in this section is vitally important, as financial institutions must evaluate loan packages based upon their underwriting standards.

8 The Uniform Residential Appraisal Report Handbook

NEIGHBORHOOD										NEIGHBORHOOD ANALYSIS	Good	Avg	Fair	Poor
LOCATION ⑤		Urban		Suburban		Rural				Employment Stability				
BUILT UP ⑥		Over 75%		25-75%		Under 25%				Convenience to Employment				
GROWTH RATE		Rapid		Stable		Slow				Convenience to Shopping				
PROPERTY VALUES		Increasing		Stable		Declining				Convenience to Schools				
DEMAND/SUPPLY		Shortage		In Balance		Over Supply				Adequacy of Public Transportation				
MARKETING TIME ⑦		Under 3 Mos.		3-6 Mos.		Over 6 Mos.				Recreation Facilities				
PRESENT LAND USE %	LAND USE CHANGE		PREDOMINANT OCCUPANCY		SINGLE FAMILY HOUSING PRICE AGE $ (000) (yrs)					Adequacy of Utilities				
Single Family	Not Likely									Property Compatibility				
2-4 Family	Likely		Owner							Protection from Detrimental Cond.				
Multi-family	In process		Tenant		Low					Police & Fire Protection				
Commercial	To:		Vacant (0-5%)		High					General Appearance of Properties				
Industrial			Vacant (over 5%)		Predominant					Appeal to Market				
Vacant					—									

Note: Race or the racial composition of the neighborhood are not considered reliable appraisal factors.
COMMENTS:

LOCATION

5. Location is a critical factor with respect to a property's value and market ability. Since financial institutions are concerned with risk, underwriters and review appraisers must be able to visualize both the neighborhood and surrounding market in order to spot healthy growth patterns versus undesirable trends that may indicate a deteriorating neighborhood with limited market appeal.

   * NOTE (Fannie Mae will purchase mortgages that are secured by residential properties in urban, suburban or rural areas.)

   * NOTE (Fannie Mae does not purchase mortgages on agricultural-type properties, on undeveloped land or on land development-type properties.)

GUIDELINE REFERENCES

Fannie Mae - January 1988 - Section 404.01 - Location

An "Urban" location relates to a city, a "Suburban" location relates to the area adjacent to a city, and a "Rural" location relates to the country or anything beyond the suburban area. To be eligible for purchase by Fannie Mae, a mortgage must be secured by a property that is residential in nature - based on the description of the subject property, zoning and the present land use.

All properties must be readily accessible by roads that meet local standards and must have adequate utilities available and in service. The appraiser must also consider the present or anticipated use of any adjoining property that may adversely effect the value or marketability of the subject property.

Certain aspects of the location of a property will require special consideration. For example, properties in resort areas that attract people for seasonal vacation use are acceptable only if they are suitable for year round use. Any property that is not suitable for year round occupancy - regardless of where it is located is unacceptable.

> **HUD - March 1987 - Exhibit 1 - Location**
> When boxes Urban and Declining are both checked, the appraiser should consider making a recommendation that the mortgage encumbering the property be insured pursuant to Section 223 (e).

BUILT UP

6. This section concerns the degree of development of a neighborhood in the percentage of the available land in the neighborhood that has been improved.

    * NOTE (Fannie Mae provides that areas that are less than 25% developed are not acceptable for maximum financing.)

    * NOTE (Fannie Mae will not purchase a mortgage that is secured by a property in a rural area or any other area that is less than 25% developed if the value of the site exceeds 30% of the total appraised value.

MARKETING TIME

7. Marketing Time is the average time that it takes for a reasonably priced property to sell in the subject neighborhood. A lengthy marketing time poses special problems as it reflects a slow market and usually declining values. Should the appraiser encounter a marketing time greater than six months, the appraiser must comment on the reason for the extended marketing period and it's effect on the property's value.

NEIGHBORHOOD ANALYSIS	Good	Avg.	Fair	Poor
Employment Stability	☐	☐	☐	☐
Convenience to Employment	☐	☐	☐	☐
Convenience to Shopping	☐	☐	☐	☐
Convenience to Schools	☐	☐	☐	☐
Adequacy of Public Transportation	☐	☐	☐	☐
Recreation Facilities	☐	☐	☐	☐
Adequacy of Utilities	☐	☐	☐	☐
Property Compatibility	☐	☐	☐	☐
Protection from Detrimental Cond.	☐	☐	☐	☐
Police & Fire Protection	☐	☐	☐	☐
General Appearance of Properties	☐	☐	☐	☐
Appeal to Market	☐	☐	☐	☐

NEIGHBORHOOD ANALYSIS

8. The appraiser is required to rate a series of factors relating to the desirability of the subject neighborhood. All fair and poor ratings in this section must be explained. Negative factors may adversely affect the value and long-term marketability of a property. The ratings on the appraisal form have been specially selected to represent items that are important to buyers in the market place. Low ratings need to be addressed since financial institutions are concerned with market strength over a long period of time.

GUIDELINE REFERENCES

Fannie Mae - January 1988 - Section 404.09 - Neighborhood Analysis Rating

The appraiser must rate the various aspects of a neighborhood by comparing the characteristics for the subject neighborhood to those for competing neighborhoods. The Appraiser must use the following ratings:

- **GOOD:** To indicate that the characteristics of the subject neighborhood are outstanding and **superior** to those found in competing neighborhoods;

- **AVERAGE:** To indicate that the characteristics of the subject neighborhood are **equal** to those that represent the "Norm" for that market area and that they are considered acceptable in competing neighborhoods;

- **FAIR:** To indicate that the characteristics of the subject neighborhood are **inferior** to those that are considered acceptable in competing neighborhoods;

- **POOR:** To indicate that the characteristics of the subject neighborhood are **substantially inferior** to - or in such small supply when compared to those found in competing neighborhoods to the point that single-family residential property values are (or may be) affected adversely.

A rating of "None" or "Non-existant" is not acceptable. The appraiser must report neighborhood conditions in factual, specific terms. The use of the ratings described above does not preclude the appraisers' reporting of typical, detrimental neighborhood condition that affect the value or marketability of the subject property.

HUD - March 1987 - Exhibit 1 - Neighborhood Analysis

Mark the most Appropriate rating for each item.

- G-Good: The item or characteristic in the subject neighborhood is **superior** to the same characteristics found in a competing neighborhood.

- A-Average: The item or characteristic is **equal** to the same characteristic found in a competing neighborhood.

- F-Fair: The item or characteristic is **below** the same characteristic found in a competing neighborhood.

- P-Poor: The item or characteristic is in **small supply** or does not exist in the subject neighborhood but is found in a competing neighborhood.

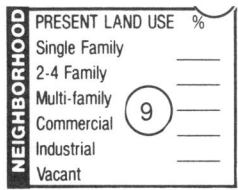

PRESENT LAND USE

9. This section shows the current use of available land in the neighborhood. The percentages of all listed should total 100%.

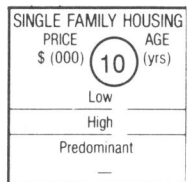

SINGLE FAMILY HOUSING

10. Residential properties that are near the top or above the top of the neighborhood value range may present a high risk to financial institutions. The Appraiser should comment on properties that are valued at 90% or more of the highest property value in the neighborhood. Such properties may represent over improvements and be difficult to sell in a reasonable length of time. The appraiser's comment can clarify whether or not a property lacks marketability because it represents an over improvement for the area.

GUIDELINE REFERENCES

Fannie Mae - January 1988 - Section 404.09 - Price Range & Predominant Price

When the subject property has a sales price (or value) that exceeds that upper price range, the property is considered as an "over-improvement" for the neighborhood. The property is considered as an "under-improvement" if its sales price (or value) is less than the lower price range. If the subject property is an over-improvement, the loan terms generally should be more conservative because the property may not be acceptable to typical purchasers. The appraiser must explain why the property is an over- or under-improvement and comment on the adjustments that were made in the "sales comparison analysis" adjustment grid to reflect that condition.

12 The Uniform Residential Appraisal Report Handbook

Note: Race or the racial composition of the neighborhood are not considered reliable appraisal factors.
COMMENTS: ⑪

COMMENTS

11. Comments in the neighborhood section must be relevant and give insight into those factors which positively or negatively affect the appraised property's marketability. A neighborhood should be acceptable to a large enough segment of buyers to support an active market. In brief, a property should have potential for long-term acceptance and be relatively free of detrimental conditions.

C. SITE SECTION

A site analysis is a collection of property data on the subject property. The appraiser should verify zoning for the subject & surrounding properties and give careful consideration to the appraisal property's highest and best use. If the improvements do not represent a legal conforming use under the current zoning classification, the appraiser must clarify whether the subject's use is "legal conforming" or "illegal". The appraiser may wish to clarify non-compliance with zoning regulation as non-compliance may have a significant impact on value and marketability.

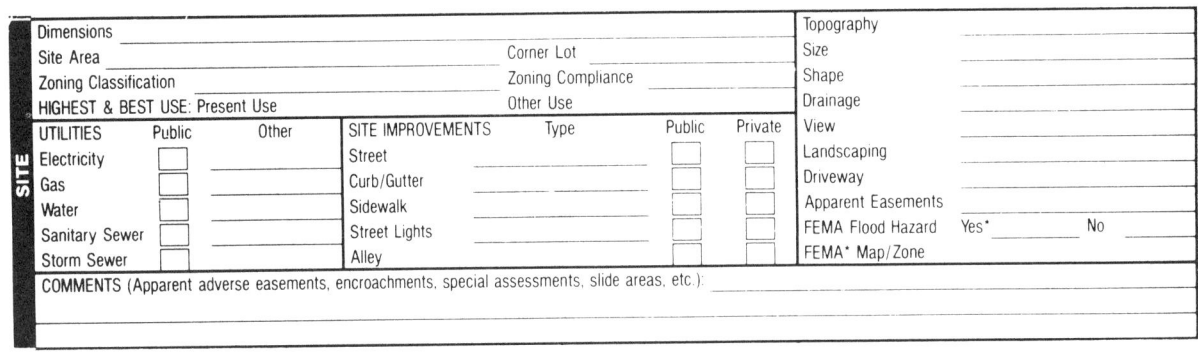

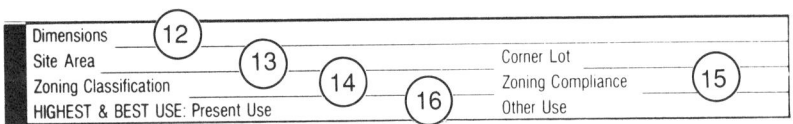

DIMENSIONS

12. All dimensions of the subject site are to be listed (width x length x width x length)

SITE AREA

13. The site should be of a size and shape that is generally conforming and acceptable in the market place.

GUIDELINE REFERENCE

> **Freddie Mac - Site** Size, shape and topography should be generally acceptable to the market - steep lot or flat lot should have comments about excess erosion or drainage.
>
> **HUD - March 1987 - Exhibit 1 - Site**
>
> Dimension: List all dimensions of the site. If irregular, the appraiser should show boundary dimensions, such as (85' x 150' x 195' x 250')
>
> Site Area: Enter area in square feet or acres
>
> Corner Lot: Enter "yes" or "no"
>
> **FMHA - March 1987 - Instructions 1922-C and 1965-A - Site Area**
>
> Enter site dimensions. If irregular enter total square footage or if more than one acre, enter the number of acres in "site area". Complete all questions.

ZONING CLASSIFICATION

14. The subject property should be assigned a specific zoning category and the type of use that is permitted by the classification.

GUIDELINE REFERENCES

> **Fannie Mae - January 1988 - Section 405.02 - Zoning**
>
> The appraiser is responsible for reporting the specific zoning classification for the subject property. The appraiser must include a general statement to describe what the zoning permits - "single-family", "two-family", etc. - when he or she indicates a specific zoning such as R-1, R-2, etc. The appraiser must also include a specific statement if the improvements do not represent a legal and conforming use of the land.
>
> **HUD - March 1988 - Exhibit I - Zoning Classification**
>
> Enter the zoning type used by the local municipality to describe the type of use permitted. Do not use abbreviations such as "R-1" or "A-1" by themselves. The abbreviated descriptions can vary among communities. For example:
>   "residential - single family"
>   "residential - 1-4 family"
> can use "Historic", if applicable.
>
> If a non-conforming use exists, enter "non-conforming" and state whether it is a legal use which has been approved by the local zoning authority. Be sure to determine if current use is in compliance.

ZONING COMPLIANCE

15. If the existing improvements do not conform to zoning regulations, the appraiser should provide a full explanation and include an estimate of the effect this has on the value of the subject property.

GUIDELINES REFERENCES

> **Fannie Mae - January 1988 - Section 405.01 - Zoning Compliance**
>
> The appraiser must also include a specific statement if the improvements do not represent a legal & Conforming use of the land.
>
> We will not purchase a mortgage on a property if the improvements do not constitute a legally permissible use of the land. We will purchase a mortgage that is secured by a property that represents a legal, but non-conforming use of the land as long as the appraiser's analysis reflects any adverse effect that the non-conforming use has on the property's value and marketability.
>
> **Freddie Mac - April 1988 - Section 2209 - Zoning Restrictions Code Requirements**
>
> **Subject property should conform to zoning requirements. However, Freddie Mac may purchase a Home Mortgage Secured by Property that does not conform to applicable zoning and use restrictions but is a "Legal use" (Legal non-conforming). Appraiser must comment on any adverse effect on any non-conforming usage when estimating the market value and marketability of the property.**
>
> **HUD - March 1988 - Exhibit 1 - Zoning Compliance**
>
> Enter "yes" or "no/legal non-conforming use". A non-conforming use could require an addendum for further explanation.

HIGHEST AND BEST USE: PRESENT USE

16. The highest and best use of a site is that reasonable and probable use that supports and the highest present value on the effective date of the appraisal. When determining a site's highest and best, each potential use must be legally permissible, financially feasible, physically and provide more profit than any other use of the site.

   * **NOTE: If the current improvement do not represent higher and best use Fannie Mae & Freddie Mac will not purchase a mortgage that is secured by the subject property.**

GUIDELINE REFERENCES

> **Fannie Mae - January 1988 - Section 405.2 - Highest and Best Use**
>
> If the use of comparable sales demonstrates that the improvements are reasonably typical and compatible with market demand for the neighborhood, and the present improvements contribute

to the value of the subject property so that its value is greater than the estimated vacant site value, the appraiser should consider the existing use as reasonable and report it as the highest and best use.

HUD - March 1987 - Exhibit - Highest and Best Use: Present Use

This entry represents the highest and best use of the site in relation to the neighborhood. If present use represents the highest and best use, enter "yes". If it does not, enter "no" and explain in the "comment" section.

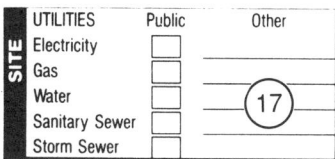

UTILITIES

17. This section identifies five categories of public or alternate utility services. If alternate are indicated, an explanation on that utility must be addressed in the "comments section".

GUIDELINE REFERENCES

Fannie Mae - January 1988 - Section 405.03 - Utilities

For a mortgage to be eligible for purchase, the security's property's utilities must met community standards and be accepted generally by area residents. If public sewer and/or water facilities - those that are supplied and regulated by the local government are not available, then community or private well and septic facilities must be available and utilitized by the subject property. Private well or septic facilities are used, the owners of the subject site. If private community facilities are used, the owners of the subject property must have the right to access the systems facilities, which must be viable on an ongoing basis.

Freddie Mac - Utilities

Must meet community standards

HUD - March 1987 - Exhibit 1 - Utilities

Either check a box or explain under "other". Public utilities are provided by a government. "Other" can reflect individual and/or community systems. Show if electricity is underground.

16 The Uniform Residential Appraisal Report Handbook

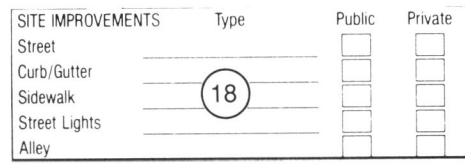

SITE IMPROVEMENTS

18. This section asks for information that is specific to the site of the particular property. The appraiser should provide a brief description on each category of improvements and mark the appropriate box if maintenance is public or private.

GUIDELINE REFERENCES

Fannie Mae - January 1988 - Section 405.04 - Streets

The property should front on a publicily dedicated and maintained street that meets community standards and is accepted generally by area residents. If the property is on a community - owned or privately owned and maintained street; there must be an adequate legally enforceable agreement for maintenance of the street. A street that does not meet city or state standards frequently requires extensive maintenance, and property values may decline if it is not regularly maintained. If a property fronts on a street that is not typical of those found in the community, the appraiser must comment on the effect of that location on the subject property's marketability and value.

HUD - March 1988 - Exhibit 1 - Site Improvements

Describe by entering either "yes" or "no" and/or a brief description under "Type" and checking whether Public or Private. For example: "Street-Asphalt; Public". It is important to identify if year-round maintenance exists. "Publix" refers to a government which can regulate use. It does not include a homeowners association.

Freddie Mac - Site Improvements

Must meet community standards. Use of private street must be legally enforceable. Charges for maintenance of private streets must be included in underwriting ratios.

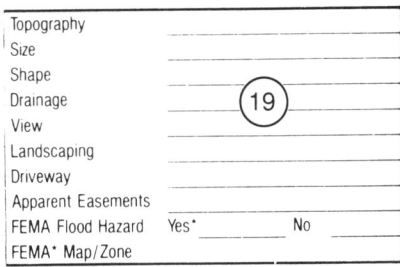

TOPOGRAPHY

19. This section is designed to describe briefly the key features of the subject site as compared with other sites within the neighborhood. Problems relating to poor drainage and/or flood conditions must be dealt with by the appraiser in the comment section or attachments. If the appraiser indicates that the property is located in a Special Flood Hazard Area - as identified by the Federal Emergency Management Agency (FEMA) - the map number and designated zone must be noted. A financial institution may need to seek additional information to determine if the degree of risk is acceptable.

   * **NOTE: You can determine whether the property is in a FEMA special flood hazard area by referencing the Floor Insurance Rate Maps (FIRM), which you can obtain from the: Federal Emergency Management Agency Flood Map Distribution Center, 6930 (A-F) San Thomas Road, Baltimore, Maryland, 211227.**

GUIDELINE REFERENCES

Fannie Mae - January 1988 - Section 405.06 - Flood Hazard Area

When the appraiser determines that a property is located in a special flood hazard area, he or she must indicate on the appraisal report form the map or community - panel number and the specific flood zone. If the appraiser indicates that the property improvements are located in a special flood hazard area - zones A, AO, AH, A1-30, A-99, V or V1-30 - flood insurance is required. If the land is in the hazard area, but the improvements are not, flood insurance is not required.

HUD - March 1988 - Exhibit 1- FEMA Hazard/FEMA Map/Zone

FEMA is the Federal Emergency Management Agency, which is responsible for mapping flood hazard areas. If any part of the property is inside a Special Flood Hazard area, check "yes". Otherwise check "no". FEMA Map/Zone: If you have checked the previous question "yes" enter map number and zone. Only those properties within zones "A" and "V" require flood insurance. Zones "B" or "C" do not require flood insurance because FEMA designates only "A" and "V" zones as "Special Flood Hazard Areas".

Freddie Mac - April 1988 - Section 2206 - Special Flood Hazard Area Designation

If propery is located in flood zone, must be checked "yes" and FEMA Map/Zone must be listed. Freddie Mac will not purchase mortgages secured by properties where the improvements are located in a flood zone without adequate Flood Hazard Insurance.

V.A. - January 1987 - Exhibit B - Part 6C "FEMA Flood Hazard"

If the appraiser indicates that the property is located in a special flood hazard area, as identified by FEMA (Federal Emergency Management Agency), the map number and designated zone must be provided.

COMMENTS (Apparent adverse easements, encroachments, special assessments, slide areas, etc.): ⑳

COMMENTS

20. Unfavorable site factors must be commented on by the appraiser. Financial institutions wish to know that site features such as size, shape and topography, etc. are acceptable in the market place. In brief, a site should meet all the criteria for a desirable lot in the area. A poor lot may result in poor marketability for the subject property. In addition, the appraisal report should explain the affect on marketability of any unfavorable site conditions such as adverse easements, encroachments or other detrimental factors.

D. IMPROVEMENT SECTION

The appraiser must provide a clear, detailed, and accurate description of the improvements. The appraiser should be as specific as possible, and should provide supporting addenda if necessary. The improvements should generally conform to the neighborhood in terms of age, type, design and materials used for their construction.

GENERAL DESCRIPTION	EXTERIOR DESCRIPTION	FOUNDATION	BASEMENT	INSULATION
Units	Foundation	Slab	Area Sq. Ft.	Roof
Stories	Exterior Walls	Crawl Space	% Finished	Ceiling
Type (Det./Att.)	Roof Surface	Basement	Ceiling	Walls
Design (Style)	Gutters & Dwnspts.	Sump Pump	Walls	Floor
Existing	Window Type	Dampness	Floor	None
Proposed ㉑	Storm Sash	Settlement	Outside Entry	Adequacy
Under Construction	Screens	Infestation		Energy Efficient Items:
Age (Yrs.)	Manufactured House			
Effective Age (Yrs.) ㉒				

PROPOSED UNDER CONSTRUCTION

21. If the appraisal of a proposed project, "yes" should be entered in the space provided. Under these conditions plans and building specifications. This would also be true if the improvements are "Under Construction".

GUIDELINES REFERENCES

Freddie Mac - Improvements

No minmum specifications for material and construction must be typical of the area.

HUD - March 1987 - Exhibit 1 - Under Construction

Enter "yes" or "no". A "yes" requires plans and specs for the appraiser to review. If REHAB Enter "Rehab" instead of "yes" or "no".

EFFECTIVE AGE (YRS.)

22. Effective age is the age indicated by the condition and design. The effective age is judgmental and may be expressed as a precise number or as a range.

GUIDELINE REFERENCES

Fannie Mae - January 1988 - Section 406.02 - Actual and Effective Ages

The relationship between the actual and effective ages of the property is a good indication of its condition. A property that has been well-maintained will generally have an effective age somewhat lower that its actual age. On the other hand, properties that have an effective age higher that their actual age probably have not been well-maintained or may have a particular physical problem. In such cases, the lender must pay particular attention to the condition of the subject property in its review of the appraisal.

HUD - March 1987 - Exhibit 1 - Effective Age (Yrs.)

Enter effective age, if appropriate. This is judgmental. May want to report a range. A differences between actual and effective age typically is caused by a level of maintenance or remodeling which may be below or above average. Significant differences between the actual and effective ages should be noted.

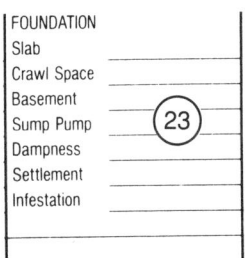

FOUNDATION

23. If there is evidence of dampness, termites or settlements, the appraiser must comment on those factors as such conditions require careful documentation. In brief, the financial institutions underwriters will have to determine the severity of the condition, etc.

GUIDELINES REFERENCES

Fannie Mae - January 1988 - Section 406.06 - Infestation, Dampness or Settlement

If the appraiser indicates that there is evidence of dampness, wood boring insects, or settlement, he or she must comment on its effect on the subject property's marketability and value. The lender must provide either satisfactory evidence that the condition was corrected or submit a professionally prepared report, which indicates that - based on an inspection of the property - the condition does not pose any threat of structural damage to the improvements.

HUD - March 1988 - Exhibit 1 - Foundation

Enter type of construction such as poured concrete, concrete block or wood.

Freddie Mac - Foundation

When evidence of dampness, settlement or infestation is present, verification that corrective action has been taken or comments on the effect on the marketability are required.

IMPROVEMENT ANALYSIS	Good	Avg	Fair	Poor
Quality of Construction				
Condition of Improvements				
Room Sizes/Layout				
Closets and Storage				
Energy Efficiency				
Plumbing-Adequacy & Condition				
Electrical-Adequacy & Condition				
Kitchen Cabinets-Adequacy & Cond.				
Compatibility to Neighborhood				
Appeal & Marketability				
Estimated Remaining Economic Life				Yrs.
Estimated Remaining Physical Life				Yrs.

(24)

IMPROVEMENT ANALYSIS

24. Fair or poor ratings for improvements must be explained. Such factors may adversely affect the property's long-term marketability. They may also limit the buyer's commitment to the property and loan.

GUIDELINES REFERENCE

Fannie Mae - January 88 - Section 407.01 - Improvement Analysis Rating

Our Appraisal report forms provide a summary of the principal factors about the improvements that have a bearing on the value and marketability of the subject property. These factors are rated to indicate how the subject property compares to competing properties in general market area. The same ratings that were used in Section 404.09 to summarize the neighborhood analysis - good, averrage, fair and poor - must be used to summarize the improvement analysis.

Freddie Mac - Improvement Analysis

Subject property improvements rated against comparable properties in subject neighborhood. Any fair or poor ratings must be satisfactorily explained.

```
┌─────────────────────────────────────────────────────────────────────────────┐
│ Additional features: ㉕                                                      │
│                                                                              │
│ Depreciation (Physical, functional and external inadequacies, repairs needed,│
│ modernization, etc.): ㉖                                                     │
│                                                                              │
│ General market conditions and prevalence and impact in subject/market area   │
│ regarding loan discounts, interest buydowns and concessions  ㉗              │
│                                                                              │
└─────────────────────────────────────────────────────────────────────────────┘
```

COMMENTS

This section is important because it provides the appraiser with an opportunity to describe any additional features not previously reported in the form; to identify any physical and functional inadequacies; and the opportunity to discuss general market conditions and the prevalence and impact on market area regarding loan discounts, interest buy downs and concessions.

ADDITIONAL FEATURES

25. Over and under improvements deserve special comments. An over improvement represents a higher risk than typical properties in the neighborhood. Further, their construction cost may be greater than their market value, Since cost and value can be quite different, the appraisers' value conclusion should reflect and be consistent with market information.

DEPRECIATION (Physical, Functional and External Inadequacies, Repairs Needed, Modernization, etc...)

26. The appraiser must comment on functional and physical inadequacies and indicate when repairs or modernization are needed. Serious attention must be given to structural problems. Unusual layouts, peculiar floor plans, inadequate equipment and amenities should be commented on. These factors limit value and market appeal and are important to the underwriter in determining the property's suitability for long-term high ratio financing.

GENERAL MARKET CONDITIONS AND PREVALENCE AND IMPACT IN SUBJECT/MARKET AREA REGARDING LOAN DISCOUNTS, INTEREST BUY DOWNS AND CONCESSIONS

27. The appraiser is expected to describe any unusual general market conditions that may affect value, such as the local economic climate and supply and demand for housing. The appraiser must identify terms, and the impact of sales in the subject market. Reviewers and underwriters are particularity interested in the appraiser's observation about the prevalence of loan discounts, interest buy downs and concessions.

V PAGE TWO OF THE UNIFORM RESIDENTIAL APPRAISAL REPORT

E. COST APPROACH SECTION

The cost approach to value assumes that a potential purchaser will consider building a substitute residence that has the same use as the property that is being appraised. This approach, then, measures value as a cost of production. The reliability of the cost approach depends on valid reproduction cost, estimates, proper depreciation estimates, and accurate site value. The cost approach is most valid in the appraisal of new or nearly new residential construction.

> * NOTE: Fannie Mae will not accept appraisals that rely solely on the cost approach as an indicator of market value.

BUILDING SKETCH

28. In estimating the cost approach, the appraiser should show measurements and state the subject's total gross living area. If the form does not provide sufficient space, the gross living area calculations can be shown on the floor plan sketch either within the cost approach section or in the exhibit section of the report.

   > * NOTE: When the appraisal is to comply with Freddie Mac or Fannie Mae requirements, this section is not for the building sketch. Freddie Mac and Fannie Mae require that this space show only square foot gross living area calculations and cost approach comments. The sketch of the building should be attached to supplement sheet.

   Typically, the square footage of the above grade living area is calculated and displayed by multiplying the exterior building dimensions, (for example, length * width) by the number of stories.

Measurements	# of Stories		Square Feet
26' x 31.33' x	1	=	815
28' x 26' x	1	=	728
2' x 7' x	1	=	14
TOTAL GROSS LIVING AREA:			1557

GUIDELINE REFERENCES

HUD - March 87 - Exhibit 1 - Cost-Approach Section

Building Sketch (Show Gross Living Area Above Grade): Sketch should include all exterior dimensions of house as well as patios, porches, garages, breeze-ways and other offsets. State "covered" or "uncovered" to indicate a roof or no roof such as over a patio.

VA - January 87 - Exhibit B - Cost Approach Section

COST APPROACH SECTION: "Building Sketch" is not required to be completed unless the appraiser needs to illustrate unique features of the subject or presence of functional obsolescence, etc.

ESTIMATED REPRODUCTION COST - NEW - OF IMPROVEMENT

29. In estimating reproduction cost, the appraiser should use cost figures that are appropriate for the local market. Further, the Appraiser should attempt to be as accurate as possible with land costs as the value of land in proportion to the value of the total property is an important underwriting consideration. The steps in the cost approach are as follows:

    • Estimate the replacement or reproduction cost new of the structure, as of the effective date of the appraisal. Total cost new includes all extras, energy-efficient items, porches, patios, etc.

- Estimate the amount of accrued depreciation categorized by physical deterioration, functional obsolescence and external obsolescence.

- Deduct accrued depreciation from total cost new to derive the depreciated value of the improvements.

- And finally, add the depreciated cost of building, improvements to the "as is" value of the site improvements to obtain the indicated total value of the subject property.

GUIDELINE REFERENCES

HUD - March 1987 - Exhibit I - Cost Approach

COST APPROACH: The estimated reproduction cost, new, of improvements, need not be completed: however, the estimated value of the site must be entered. If the subject property is proposed construction or existing construction under one year of age, the Marshall and Swift Form 1007 is to be completed and attached, in conformance with Deputy Assistant Secretary Nistler's Memorandum of Instructions dated December 17, 1985.

VA - January 1987 - Exhibit B - Cost Approach Cost

COST APPROACH SECTION: Only the "Estimated Site Value" must be completed in every case proposed or existing (condominiums excluded).

Freddie Mac - April 87 - Section 2201 (b)- Cost Approach

Freddie Mac prefers to see cost approach. If not applicable, we must at least have "estimated site value".

Must included adjustments for items adversely affecting marketability such as physical, functional and/or external depreciation as well as explanations thereof.

Fannie Mae - January 1987 - Section 408.01 - Cost Approach

If the appraiser's estimate of the value for the site is one that is not typical for a comparable residential property in the subject neighborhood, he or she must comment on how the variance affects the marketability of the subject property.

F. SALES COMPARISON ANALYSIS

Analysis of market data is essential to the valuation of all single-family residential properties. The sales comparison approach employs the principle of substitutional or the substitution of alternative properties for the subject as the basis of the determination of value.

The sales comparison analysis begins with the selection of a relevant subset of similar properties. This subset may range from one to several hundred. All based on this criteria, the comparable sales selected should only include those sales that demonstrate similarities to the subject property, although the Uniform Residential Appraisal Report form allows room for only three comparable sales, the appraiser in all cases should include as many sales necessary to support and substantiate the value estimate. The additional sales can be attached in an addendum. Adjustments are then made, via market observation by comparing components of the selected market sales to the subject property.

The undersigned has recited three recent sales of properties most similar and proximate to subject and has considered these in the market analysis. The description includes a dollar adjustment, reflecting market reaction to those items of significant variation between the subject and comparable properties. If a significant item in the comparable property is superior to, or more favorable than, the subject property, a minus (−) adjustment is made, thus reducing the indicated value of subject; if a significant item in the comparable is inferior to, or less favorable than, the subject property, a plus (+) adjustment is made, thus increasing the indicated value of the subject.

ITEM	SUBJECT	COMPARABLE NO. 1		COMPARABLE NO. 2		COMPARABLE NO. 3	
Address							
Proximity to Subject							
Sales Price	$		$		$		$
Price/Gross Liv. Area	$	$		$		$	
Data Source							
VALUE ADJUSTMENTS	DESCRIPTION	DESCRIPTION	+(−)$ Adjustment	DESCRIPTION	+(−)$ Adjustment	DESCRIPTION	+(−)$ Adjustment
Sales or Financing Concessions							
Date of Sale/Time							
Location							
Site/View							
Design and Appeal							
Quality of Construction							
Age							
Condition							
Above Grade Room Count	Total / Bdrms / Baths	Total / Bdrms / Baths		Total / Bdrms / Baths		Total / Bdrms / Baths	
Gross Living Area	Sq. Ft.	Sq. Ft.		Sq. Ft.		Sq. Ft.	
Basement & Finished Rooms Below Grade							
Functional Utility							
Heating/Cooling							
Garage/Carport							
Porches, Patio, Pools, etc.							
Special Energy Efficient Items							
Fireplace(s)							
Other (e.g. kitchen equip., remodeling)							
Net Adj. (total)		□ + □ −	$	□ + □ −	$	□ + □ −	$
Indicated Value of Subject			$		$		$

Comments on Sales Comparison: _____

SELECTING COMPARABLES

Proximity to the subject property is an important point the the selection of comparable properties. The appraiser should select sales within the subject neighborhood in order to avoid adjustments for location differences. The sales price of the comparables must be verified and must be recently closed sales of similar properties. The appraiser should avoid using old comparables. Sales should have occurred with in the last six months. Any sales that are over six months old must be explained. Markets change, and sometimes swiftly. Therefore, it is important the appraisers use the most recent sales available.

GUIDELINES RFERENCES

> **Fannie Mae - January 1988 - Section 408.02 - Sales comparison Approach**
>
> A. Selecting the comparables. The appraiser must report a minimum of three comparable sales as part of the sales comparison approach. The appraiser may submit more than three comparable sales to support his or her estimate of market value, as long as at least three are actual settled or closed sales. Generally, the appraiser should use comparable sales that have been settled or closed within the last 12 months. However, the appraiser must submit on the reasons for using any comparable sales that are more than six months old. In additin, the appraiser may use the subject property as a fourth comparable sale of as supporting data if the property previously was sold (and closed or settled). If the appraiser believes that it is appropriate, he or she also may use contract offerings and current listings as supporting data.
>
> **HUD - March 1987 - Exhibit I - Sales Comparison**
>
> PROXIMITY TO SUBJECT : Enter proximity "as the crow flies." Enter description like "3 houses W subject." If comparable is more than 1 mile from subject, be sure to explain in the "Comments" section.
>
> **Freddie Mac - April 87 - Section 220/ (c) - Sales Comparison Approach**
>
> The value indicated by the sales comparison approach must be supported by an analysis of sales of at least three comparable properties. The comparable properties should have the following characteristics:
> - located near the subject property
> - recently sold
> - closing/settlement has occurred

ADJUSTMENTS TO COMPARABLE SALES

The appraiser should attempt to "bracket" the sales data before making adjustments. In brief, the appraiser should find properties that are a little better than the subject and those that are not quite as good, as well as a range in between. This will enable the appraiser to establish a tight value range. Proper bracketing aids the appraiser in producing a convincing appraisal report.

Comparable sales data should be adjusted to the subject property - except for sales and financing, concessions, which are adjusted to the market at the time sale. Normally, adjustments are based on percentages with the resulting dollar figure rounded to the nearest $100, $500, or $1000, depending on the market.

When making adjustments, keep in mind the following:

- The comparables must be adjusted to the effective date of the appraisal.
- The subject is the standard by which the comparable sales are evaluated & adjusted.
- Adjustments should be made from market data (supported by documented market evidence)

- All adjustments to the Comparable Sales for items that are superior are adjusted with a negative (−) dollar adjustment and all inferior items with a positive (+) dollar adjustment.

Finally, appraisers must not engage in excessive adjusting. Large adjustments indicate that the comps are not comparable. Large upward adjustments reveal to the Review Appraiser or Mortgage Underwriter that the appraiser is pumping value. Gross adjustments should not exceed 25% of the comparable sales price. Individual line adjustments must not be greater than 10% of the sales prices. In brief, the appraiser's adjustments should be realistic.

   * **Note: Adjustment parameter vary from one agency to another**

GUIDELINE REFERENCES

Fannie Mae - January 1988 - Section 408.02

B. Adjustments to comparable sales. Each comparable sale that is used in the sales comparison approach must be analyzed for differences and similarities between it and the property that is being appraised. The appraiser must make appropriate adjustments for location, terms and condition of sale, date of sale, and the physical characteristics of the properites.

"Time" adjustments must be representative of the market and should be supported by the comparable sales whenevers possible. The adjustments must reflect the time that elapsed between the contract date (or the date of the "meeting of the minds") for the comparable sale and the effective date of the appraisal for the subject property.

Comparable sales must be adjusted to the subject property - except for sales and financing concessions, which are adjusted to the market at the time of sale. The subject property is the standard against which the comparable sales are evaluated and adjusted. Thus, if an item in the comparable property is superior to that in the subject property, a minus (−) adjustment is required to make that item equal to that in the subject property. Conversely, if an item in the comparable property is inferior to that in the subject property, a plus (+) adjustment is required to make that item equal to that in the subject property.

HUD - March 1988 - Exhibit A - Sales Comparison Analysis

Always select the comparables with the fewest dissimilarities. Use older sales only if more recent ones are not available and be sure to explain their use in the "Comments" section.

The value factors of Location, Site/View, Design and Appeal, Quality of Construction, Age, Condition, and Functional Utility are all subjective factors that require subjective adjustments. Be careful that your adjustments are reasonable - not excessive. If a property is ever over-valued, a high probablility exists that the reason can be traced to an excessive adjustment somewhere in this section.

Freddie Mac - Sales Comparison Analysis

All adjustments should reflect what typical buyers in the market place are paying for certain elements. Such adjustments should not necessarily represent pre-selected cost data.

> Significant adjustments for location, site/view, design/appeal and quality of construction should be explained in the "comment" section.
>
> Suggested guidelines for maximum adjustments are 10% per line and 15% gross adjustment, where insufficient market data is avialable, explain reasoning from comparables chosen and address impact on reliability of value.
>
> **FmHa - May 1987 - Sales Comparison Analysis**
>
> Net Adjustments normally should not exceed 15% of the sales prices. Gross adjustments normally should not exceed 25% of the sales price.

VALUE ADJUSTMENTS	DESCRIPTION	DESCRIPTION	+ (-) $ Adjustment	DESCRIPTION	+ (-) $ Adjustment	DESCRIPTION	+ (-) $ Adjustment
Sales or Financing Concessions		(30)					

SALES OR FINANCING CONCESSIONS

30. The appraiser must take into account concessions and financing involved in each of the comparable transactions and apply it to what is typical in the market. If the appraisal of the subject property is connected with a sale, the final valuation must be contingent upon the financing or concession utilized in that transaction, if not typical of the market. The appraiser must explore the possibilities of another sale occurring under those same conditions. If the possibilities remote the appraiser must adjust for the terms of the sale. Review Appraisers and Morgage Underwriters pay close attention to these factors in periods of "tight money".

GUIDELINES REFERENCES

> **Fannie Mae - January 1988 - Section 408.02 - Sales Comparison Analysis**
>
> Sales or financing concessions. The dollar amount of sales or financing concessions paid by the seller must be reported for the comparables if the information is reasonably available. Generally, sales or financing data for comparable sales - such as the mortgage amount, loan type, interest rate, term, and any fees or concessions the seller paid - is available. The appraiser should obtain this information from an individual who was party to the comparable transaction (the broker, buyer, or seller) or from a data source that the appraisers considers to be reliable. We recognize that there may be some situations in which sales or financing information is not available because of legal restrictions or other disclosure - related problems. In such cases, the appraiser must explain why the information is not available - however, we will not accept an explanation that indicates that the appraiser did not make an effort to verify the information. In all other cases, the appraiser must provide the sales and financing concession information that was available (and verified) for the comparables. If the appraisal report form does not provide enough space to discuss this information, the appraiser should make adjustments for the concessions on the form and explain them in an addendum to the appraisal report.

Examples of sales or financing concessions include interest rate buy downs or other below market rate financing; loan discount points; loan origination fees; closing customarily paid by the buyer; payment of condominum or PUD association fees; refunds of (or credit for) the borrower's expenses; absorption of monthly payments; and the inclusion of non-reality items in the transaction. The amount of the negative adjustment to be made to each comparable with sales or financing concessions is equal to any increase in the purchase price of the comparable that the appraiser determines to be attributable to the concessions.

The need to make negative adjustments and the amount of the adjustments to the comparables for sales and financing concessions are not based on how typical the concessions might be for a segment of the market area - large sales concessions can be relatively typical in a particular segment of the market and still result in sale prices that reflect more than the value of the real estate. Adjustments based on mechanical, dollar-for-dollar, deductions that are equal to the cost of the concessions to the seller (as a strict cash equivalency approach would dictate) are not appropriate. We recognize that the effect of the sales concessions on sales prices can vary with the amount of the concessions and differences in various markets. The adjustments must reflect the differences between what the comparables actually sold for with the sales concessions and what they would have sold for without the concessions so that the dollar amount of the adjustments will approximate the market's reaction to the concession.

Positive adjustments for sales or financing concessions are not acceptable. For example, if local tradition or law results in virtually all of the property sellers in the market area paying a 1% loan origination fee for the purchaser, and a property seller in that market did not pay any loan fees or concessions for the purchaser, the sale would be considered as a cash equivalent sale in that market. The appraiser should recognize comparable sales that sold for all cash or with cash equivalent financing and use them as comparables if they are the best indicators of value for the subject property. Such sales can also be useful to the appraiser in determining those costs that are normally paid by sellers as the result of tradition or law in the market area.

HUD - March 87 Exhibit 1 - Sales or Financing Concessions

The adjustment for sales or financing concessions is done here, if applicable. Each comparable is adjusted in accordance with instructions continued in Mortgage Letter 86 -15. Be sure to explain in Comments on Sales Comparison Section and use an addendum if appropriate.

VA - February 87 - Paragraph 6f - Sales or Financing Concessions

The appraiser must consider & report the effect of any sales or financing incentives involved in the comparable sales transaction. Fee appraisers are directed to local release #86-18 (DVB Circular 26 - 86 - 9, Par 4f) which states VA's policy regarding seller incentives.

Freddie Mac - January 87 - Section 2215 - Market Value

Adjustments to the comparables must be made for special or creative financing or sales concessions. No adjustments are necessary for those costs which are normally paid by sellers as a result of tradition or law in a market area; these costs are readily identifiable since the seller pays these costs in virtually all sales transactions. Special or creative financing adjustments can be made to the comparable property by comparisons to financing terms offered by a third - party institutional

32 The Uniform Residential Appraisal Report Handbook

> lender that is not already involved in the property or transaction. Any adjustment should not be calculated on a mechanical dollar - for dollar cost of the financing or concession but the dollar amount of any adjustment should approximate the market's reaction ot the financing or concessions based on the appraiser's judgement.

VALUE ADJUSTMENTS	DESCRIPTION	DESCRIPTION	+(-) $ Adjustment	DESCRIPTION	+(-) $ Adjustment	DESCRIPTION	+(-) $ Adjustment
Sales or Financing Concessions							
Date of Sale/Time	(31)						

DATE OF SALES/TIME ADJUSTMENT

31. All comparable sales must be recently closed sales (closed within the past 12 months). Using sales more than six months old should be explained. Time adjustments must reflect the market. The Appraiser should avoid making upward adjustment in a declining market.

GUIDELINE REFERENCES

Fannie Mae January 85 - Section 408.02 - Sales Comparison Analysis

We will accept more than three comparable sales as part of the appraisal report, but at least three of them must be actual settled or closed sales. The appraiser should provide the date of the sales contract and the settlement or closing date for each comparable sale. Unless the appraiser believes that the exact date is necessary to understand the adjustments, only the month and year of the sale need to be reported. If the appraiser does not report both the contract date and the settlement or closing date, he or she must identify the reported sale date as either the "contract date" or the "settlement or closing date". If the appraiser reports the contract date only, he or she must state whether the contract resulted in a settlement of a closing.

HUD March 88 - Exhibit I - Sales Comparison Analysis

Date of Sale/Time: Enter month and year. This date refers to a date of closing. A specific day is not necessary unless it is meaningful, such as in a rapidly changing market.

NET ADJUSTMENTS

32. The net adjustment section is used to report the net total position (+) or negative (−) adjustments for all items. Excessive adjustments indicate that the comps. are not comparable.

GUIDELINES REFERENCES

Fannie Mae - January 88 - Section 408.02 - Sales Comparison Analysis

We have established guidelines for the net and gross percentage adjustments that underwriters may rely on as a general indicator of whether a property should be used as a comparable sale. Generally, the dollar amount of the net adjustments for each comparable sale should not exceed 15%, the appraiser must comment on the reasons for not using a more similar comparable. Further, the dollar amount of the gross adjustments for each comparable. Further, the dollar amount of the gross adjustments for each comparable sale should not exceed 25% of the comparable's sales price. The amount of the gross adjustments determined by adding all individual adjustments without regarding to the plus or minus signs. When the adjustments exceed 25%, the appraiser must comment on the reasons for not using a more similar comparable. Individual adjustments that are excessively high should be explained by the appraiser and reviewed carefully by the lender's underwriter. In some circumstances, the use of comparables with higher-than-normal adjustments may be warranted, but the appraiser must satisfactorily justify his or her use of them.

The appraiser must research the market and select the most comparable sales that are available for the subject property, and then adjust them to reflect the market's reaction to the differences (except for sales and financing concessions) between the comparable sales and the subject property, without regard for the percentage or amount of the dollar adjustments. If the appraiser's adjustments do not fall within our net and gross percentage adjustment guidelines, but the appraiser believes that the comparable sales used in the analysis are the best available, as well as the best indicators of value for the subject property, appraiser simply has to provide an appropriate explanation. If the extent of the appraiser's adjustments to the comparable sales is great enough to indicate that the property may not conform to the general market area, the lenders underwriter must give special consideration to the case. An atypical property might require more conservative mortgage terms because it might not be appealing to a typical purchaser in the market area.

HUD - March 87 - Exhibit I - Net Adjustment Total

Check either (+) or (−) box to indicate if the total net adjustments will increase or decrease the sales price. If any adjustment is excessive, the comparables should be reviewed to determine if the best one were selected. Any adjustment which appears to be excessive should be explained.

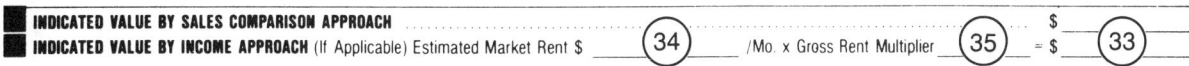

INDICATED VALUE BY INCOME APPROACH

33. The Income Approach is a misnomer when applied to the residential market. If rents on Single Family Residences are available, this actually market determined through the gross rent multiplies approach.

ESTIMATED MARKET RENT

34. The estimated monthly rent that the subject could be expected to generate if leased, should be calculated and recorded in this space.

GROSS RENT MULTIPLIER

35. GRM (Gross Rent Multiplier) may be applied either to a monthly market rent or to a annual rent, and is determined by dividing the sales price of a comparable by it's monthly or annual rent.

GUIDELINES REFERENCES

Fannie Mae - January 88 - Section 408.03 - Income Approach

The income approach to value is based on the assumption that market value is related to the market rent or income that a property can be expected to earn. Its use generally is appropriated in neighborhoods of single-family properties when there is a substantial rental market, and it is an important approach in the valuation of a two or four family property. However, it generally is not appropriate in areas that consist mostly of owner-occupied properties since adequate rental data generally does not exist for those areas. We will not accept an appraisal if the appraiser relies solely on the income approach as an indicator of market value.

To arrive at the indicated value by the income approach, the appraiser multiplies the estimated market rent for the subject property by a gross rent multiplier.

- **Estimated market rent** is based on an analysis of comparable rentals in the neighborhood. After appropriate adjustments are made to the comparables, their adjusted (or indicated) values are reconciled to develop an estimated monthly market rent for the subject property.

- **The gross rent multiplier** is determined by dividing the sales price of comparable properties that were rented at the time of sale by their monthly market rent, whic is then reconciled to creat a single gross rent multiplier (or a range of multipliers) for the subject property.

When the property being appraised is a single-family property that will be used as an investment property, the appraiser must prepare a Single-Family Comparable Rent Schedule (Form 1007) in addition to the appropriate appraisal report form. This form is not required for a two to four family property since the Appraisal Report-Small Residential Income Property (Form 1025) provides substantially the same information. When the appraiser is relying on the income approach, he or she should attach the supporting comparable rental and sales data, and the calculations used to determine the gross rent multiplier, as an addendum to the appraisal report form.

Freddie Mac - April 87 - Section 220/ (d) - Income Approach

The value indicated by the income approach, if considered applicable by the appraiser, must be derived by the gross rent multiplier technique using market rent. For nonowner - occupied (NOO) investment properties, the appraiser must use the income approach and support the market rent used in the appraisal.

HUD - March 88 Exhibit I - Income Approach

The Income Approach need be completed only for three and four unit properties. When used, the appraiser is to show the gross rent form each of the comparables at the bottom of the form under "Final Reconciliation" as: comp. #1 Gross Rent = $1,000.00 Comp. #2 Gross Rent = 1,200.00 . . . .", etc.

If the Income Approach is not used, the appraiser should draw a line through the words "Indicated Value by Income Approach (if applicable)" and enter the estimated market rent. The rest of the line items should be marked "N/A."

Check the box marked "as is" or "subject to repairs.."

VA - February 87 - Paragraph 7d - Indicated Value by Income Approach

This section will be completed only if applicable and a valid indicator of value (e.g., multi-unit building).

G. RECONCILIATION SECTION

The reconciliation section, the appraiser evaluates and reconciles each approach to value in arriving at a final estimate of market value. In the section, the appraiser has the final opportunity to discuss the subject property and the application of all approaches to value.

Final Reconciliation

36. This section allows the appraiser to explain the relevance and validity of each valuation approach and justify the final value estimate. The appraiser will check the appropriate boxes and complete the comments and reconciliation sections under the sales comparison grid. The appraisal must be based on the definition of market value that is stated in the must be based on the definition of market value that is stated the certification and Statement of limiting conditions that are stated in:
    FMHA, HUD and or VA Instructions
    Freddie Mac Form 439 (Rev. 7/88)/Fannie Mac Form 1004B (Rev 7/86) filed with clients

36 The Uniform Residential Appraisal Report Handbook

GUIDELINES REFERENCES

> ### Fannie Mae - January 88 - Section 409 - Final Reconciliation
>
> The reconciliation process that leads to the estimate of market value is an on-going process throughout the appraiser's analysis. In the final reconciliation, the appraiser must reconcile the reasonableness and reliability of each approach to value and the reasonableness and validity of the indicated values and the available data, and then must select and report the approach or approaches that were given the most weight. The final reconciliation must never be an averaging technique.
>
> If the appraiser has provided a comprehensive and logical analysis of the neighborhood and the property, the lender's underwriter should be able to reach a sound conclusion on the adequacy of the property as security for the mortgage.
>
> We will not purchase a mortgage unless the appraisal is based on our Certification and Statement of Limited Conditions (Form 1004B) as it was revised in July, 1986. To acknowledge that the current version of the Form 1004B was used and to assure the lender that the appraiser is certifying to our current definition of value, the appraiser must.
>
> Check the box in the Form 1004B was used and to assure the lender that the appraiser is certifying to our current definition of value, the appraiser must.
>
> Check the box in the "Reconciliation" section of the Uniform Residential Appraisal Report (Form 1004) that references "Freddie Mac Form 439 (Rev. 7/86), Fannie Mae Form 1004B (Rev 7/86) ....";or
>
> Check the box at the bottom of the Appraisal Report - Small Residential Income Property (Form 1025), the Appraisal Report-Individual condominium or PUD Unit (Form 1073), or the Loan Valuation Summary for Second Mortgages (Form 219), that references the Freddie Mac Form 439/Fannie Mae Form 1004B , and correct any references to the out dated version of Form 1004B by striking the earlier revision date and replacing it with a "07/86" date.
>
> ### HUD - March 87 - Exhibit I - Final Reconciliation
>
> This entry should contain the appraiser's reasoning for arriving at the final value. The appraiser must sign his/her name, print name under signature with assigned CHUMS identification number and date report as of the day inspected. The Reviewer also signs, dates and writes CHUMS identification number at the bottom of the report as of date review and then completes the Data Entry Sheet.

Certification Signature Lines

37. The appraiser should type his or her name under the signature line. By his or her signature, the appraiser certifies the personal inspection of the Interior and Exterior of the subject propety and the exteriors of all comparable sale properties.

Conclusion

The appraisal report should give a concise and precise picture of the neighborhood, site, improvements, value and marketability of the subject property. Backing into the approaches to value, based upon the sales price of the subject, is unacceptable appraisal practice. Value is not intrinsic to the property being appraised but is derived from what other similar properties in the subject neighborhood have sold for recently. In brief, sales price and market value are two different concepts.

VI Documentation in Support of the Uniform Residential Report

Required Documentation in support of the Uniform Residential Appraisal Report include:

Clear, descriptive photographs that show the front of each comparable property. The appropriate property address should be indicated on each photograph;

Clear, descriptive photographs that show the front and back of the subject property, as well as one that shows a street scene;

A floor plan sketch that identifies and shows the location of all rooms, interior walls, and interior and exterior doors. Although the floor plan sketch should closely resemble the subject property, it does not need to be drawn to scale;

An area map that shows the location of the subject property and of all comparables that the appraiser used;

Single Family Comparable Rent Schedule for single-family investment properties if the property is rented;

Certificate of Completion & Recertification of Value (if applicable) and;

Any other data that is necessary to provide a complete appraisal report.

VII A Uniform Residential Appraisal Report Case Study with Attachments

UNIFORM RESIDENTIAL APPRAISAL REPORT

Property Description & Analysis

File No. _____

SUBJECT
- Property Address: 16418 North 67th Street
- Census Tract: 1032.1327
- City: Scottsdale County: Maricopa State: Az. Zip Code: 85254
- Legal Description: lot 73, Country Trace
- Owner/Occupant: Brown, Stephen L.
- Map Reference: 215-40-188
- Sale Price $ _____ Date of Sale _____
- Property Rights Appraised: [X] Fee Simple, [ ] Leasehold, [ ] Condominium (HUD/VA), [ ] De Minimis PUD
- Loan charges/concessions to be paid by seller $ _____
- R.E. Taxes $ 875.86 Tax Year 88 HOA $/Mo. N/A
- Lender/Client: Valley View Bank, 10325 E. Shea Blvd., Scottsdale, Az.

LENDER DISCRETIONARY USE
- Sale Price $ _____
- Date _____
- Mortgage Amount $ _____
- Mortgage Type _____
- Discount Points and Other Concessions Paid by Seller $ _____
- Source _____

NEIGHBORHOOD

						NEIGHBORHOOD ANALYSIS	Good	Avg.	Fair	Poor
LOCATION	[ ] Urban	[X] Suburban	[ ] Rural			Employment Stability	X			
BUILT UP	[ ] Over 75%	[X] 25-75%	[ ] Under 25%			Convenience to Employment		X		
GROWTH RATE	[ ] Rapid	[X] Stable	[ ] Slow			Convenience to Shopping		X		
PROPERTY VALUES	[ ] Increasing	[X] Stable	[ ] Declining			Convenience to Schools		X		
DEMAND/SUPPLY	[ ] Shortage	[X] In Balance	[ ] Over Supply			Adequacy of Public Transportation		X		
MARKETING TIME	[ ] Under 3 Mos.	[X] 3-6 Mos.	[ ] Over 6 Mos.			Recreation Facilities		X		

PRESENT LAND USE %: Single Family 70, 2-4 Family __, Multi-family __, Commercial __, Industrial __, Vacant 30

LAND USE CHANGE: [ ] Not Likely [X], [ ] Likely, [ ] In process, To: _____

PREDOMINANT OCCUPANCY: [X] Owner, [ ] Tenant, [X] Vacant (0-5%), [ ] Vacant (over 5%)

SINGLE FAMILY HOUSING PRICE $(000) / AGE (yrs): 80 Low New, 155 High 5, Predominant 90–125

Adequacy of Utilities: X Avg; Property Compatibility: X Avg; Protection from Detrimental Cond.: X Avg; Police & Fire Protection: X Avg; General Appearance of Properties: X Avg; Appeal to Market: X Avg

Note: Race or the racial composition of the neighborhood are not considered reliable appraisal factors.

COMMENTS: Above average tract home subdivision located in Northeast Phoenix area Southeast of the intersection of Bell Road and 64th Street. Schools and Shopping Centers are in close proximity. Marketability in this area is good. Good residential Neighborhood.

SITE
- Dimensions: 118 x 17 x 100 x 80
- Site Area: 8,650 ±
- Corner Lot: No
- Zoning Classification: R1-8 Sgl Family Res Zoning Compliance: In Compl.
- HIGHEST & BEST USE: Present Use Residential Other Use _____
- Topography: Level
- Size: Normal
- Shape: Rectangular
- Drainage: Adequate
- View: Normal
- Landscaping: Mature
- Driveway: Concrete
- Apparent Easements: Utility
- FEMA Flood Hazard Yes* __ No No
- FEMA* Map/Zone _____

UTILITIES: Electricity Public X; Gas X; Water X; Sanitary Sewer X; Storm Sewer X

SITE IMPROVEMENTS: Street Asphalt (Public X); Curb/Gutter Yes (Public X); Sidewalk Concrete (Public X); Street Lights Yes (Public X); Alley N/A

COMMENTS: No adverse easements, encroachments or conditions noted. Good Residential Site.

IMPROVEMENTS

GENERAL DESCRIPTION:
- Units: One
- Stories: One
- Type (Det./Att.): Detached
- Design (Style): Ranch
- Existing: Yes
- Proposed: No
- Under Construction: No
- Age (Yrs.): 4
- Effective Age (Yrs.): 2-3

EXTERIOR DESCRIPTION:
- Foundation: Concrete
- Exterior Walls: Block
- Roof Surface: Asph. Shg
- Gutters & Dwnspts.: Partial
- Window Type: Alum. Slid
- Storm Sash: No
- Screens: Yes
- Manufactured House: No

FOUNDATION:
- Slab: Concrete
- Crawl Space: None
- Basement: None
- Sump Pump: None
- Dampness: N/A
- Settlement: N/A
- Infestation: N/A

BASEMENT:
- Area Sq. Ft.: N/A
- % Finished: N/A
- Ceiling: N/A
- Walls: N/A
- Floor: N/A
- Outside Entry: N/A

INSULATION: Roof X; Ceiling X; Walls X; Floor N/A; None N/A; Adequacy Avg X; Energy Efficient Items: _____

ROOM LIST

ROOMS	Foyer	Living	Dining	Kitchen	Den	Family Rm.	Rec. Rm.	Bedrooms	# Baths	Laundry	Other	Area Sq. Ft.
Basement												
Level 1	1	1	1	1		1		3	2			
Level 2												

Finished area above grade contains: 7 Rooms; 3 Bedroom(s); 2 Bath(s); 1557 Square Feet of Gross Living Area

INTERIOR

SURFACES:
- Floors: Carpt/Mex. Tile
- Walls: Drywall
- Trim/Finish: Oak
- Bath Floor: Vinyl
- Bath Wainscot: Ceramic Tile
- Doors: Wood, Ceiling Fan
- Fireplace(s): None #

HEATING: Type Ht Pump; Fuel Elect.; Condition Good; Adequacy Avg.

COOLING: Central Yes; Other _____; Condition Good; Adequacy Avg.

KITCHEN EQUIP.: Refrigerator None; Range/Oven X; Disposal X; Dishwasher X; Fan/Hood X; Compactor; Washer/Dryer; Microwave X; Intercom

ATTIC: None; Stairs; Drop Stair; Scuttle X; Floor; Heated; Finished

IMPROVEMENT ANALYSIS (Good / Avg / Fair / Poor):
- Quality of Construction: X
- Condition of Improvements: X
- Room Sizes/Layout: X
- Closets and Storage: X
- Energy Efficiency: X
- Plumbing-Adequacy & Condition: X
- Electrical-Adequacy & Condition: X
- Kitchen Cabinets-Adequacy & Cond.: X
- Compatibility to Neighborhood: X
- Appeal & Marketability: X
- Estimated Remaining Economic Life: 50-60 Yrs.
- Estimated Remaining Physical Life: 50-60 Yrs.

CAR STORAGE
- Garage: [X] Attached [X]
- No. Cars: 2
- Carport: [ ] Detached [ ]
- Condition: Ab Avg [ ] None [ ] Built-In [ ] Electric Door
- House Entry: X; Outside Entry: X; Basement Entry: _____

COMMENTS

Additional features: Walk-In closet, wood shutters, vaulted ceiling, ceramic kitchen countertops, track lighting in kitchen, block fence, underground sprinklers heating s/c pool & spa, 8x16 wood deck, covered patio & garden window

Depreciation (Physical, functional and external inadequacies, repairs needed, modernization, etc.):
No Physical or functional inadequacies.

General market conditions and prevalence and impact in subject/market area regarding loan discounts, interest buydowns and concessions:
Typical sales marketing in this general area good.

Freddie Mac Form 70 10/86   U.S. Forms Inc. 2 Central Sq. Grafton, MA 01519-0446, 1-800-225-9583   Fannie Mae Form 1004 10/86

UNIFORM RESIDENTIAL APPRAISAL REPORT

Valuation Section — File No. _____

Purpose of Appraisal is to estimate Market Value as defined in the Certification & Statement of Limiting Conditions.

COST APPROACH

BUILDING SKETCH (SHOW GROSS LIVING AREA ABOVE GRADE)
If for Freddie Mac or Fannie Mae show only square foot calculations and cost approach comments in this space

```
26 X 31.33 X 1        =  815
28 X 26    X 1        =  728
 2 X  7    X 1        =   14
           Total Sq. Ft. = 1557

*Attached Sketch
```

(Not Required by Freddie Mac and Fannie Mae)
Does property conform to applicable HUD/VA property standards? [X] Yes [ ] No
If No, explain: _____

ESTIMATED REPRODUCTION COST – NEW – OF IMPROVEMENTS:

Dwelling 1557 Sq. Ft. @ $ 39.50	= $	61,501.
N/A Sq. Ft. @ $	=	
Extras	=	12,500.
	=	1,750.
Special Energy Efficient Items	=	
Porches, Patios, etc.	=	3,500.
Garage/Carport Sq. Ft. @ $	=	6,762.
Total Estimated Cost New	= $	86,013.
Less Depreciation: Physical / Functional / External	= $	2,580.
Depreciated Value of Improvements	= $	83,433.
Site Imp. "as is" (driveway, landscaping, etc.)	= $	10,000.
ESTIMATED SITE VALUE	= $	32,000.
(If leasehold, show only leasehold value.)		
INDICATED VALUE BY COST APPROACH	= $	125,400.

Construction Warranty [ ] Yes [X] No
Name of Warranty Program _____
Warranty Coverage Expires _____

SALES COMPARISON ANALYSIS

The undersigned has recited three recent sales of properties most similar and proximate to subject and has considered these in the market analysis. The description includes a dollar adjustment, reflecting market reaction to those items of significant variation between the subject and comparable properties. If a significant item in the comparable property is superior to, or more favorable than, the subject property, a minus (–) adjustment is made, thus reducing the indicated value of subject; if a significant item in the comparable is inferior to, or less favorable than, the subject property, a plus (+) adjustment is made, thus increasing the indicated value of the subject.

ITEM	SUBJECT	COMPARABLE NO. 1	+(–)$ Adj	COMPARABLE NO. 2	+(–)$ Adj	COMPARABLE NO. 3	+(–)$ Adj
Address	16418 N. 67th St.	6707 E. Grandview		6613 E. Kings Ave		6610 E. Kings Ave	
Proximity to Subject		same subdivision		same subdivision		same subdivision	
Sales Price	$	$125,000		$126,000		$124,000	
Price/Gross Liv. Area	$	$80.28		$80.92		$79.64	
Data Source	Inspection	MLS/Broker		MLS/Broker		MLS/Broker	
VALUE ADJUSTMENTS	DESCRIPTION	DESCRIPTION		DESCRIPTION		DESCRIPTION	
Sales or Financing Concessions		New Conv.		VA		New Conv.	
Date of Sale/Time	Current	3/88		1/88		2/88	
Location	Above Avg.	Equal		Equal		Equal	
Site/View	Above Avg.	Equal		Equal		Equal	
Design and Appeal	Above Avg.	Equal		Equal		Equal	
Quality of Construction	Above Avg.	Equal		Equal		Equal	
Age	4	Equal		Equal		Equal	
Condition	Above Avg.	Equal		Equal		Equal	+1500
Above Grade Room Count	Total 7 / Bdrms 3 / Baths 2	7 / 3 / 2		7 / 3 / 2		7 / 3 / 2	
Gross Living Area	1557 Sq.Ft.	1557 Sq.Ft.		1557 Sq.Ft.		1557 Sq.Ft.	
Basement & Finished Rooms Below Grade	N/A	N/A		N/A		N/A	
Functional Utility	Adequate	Equal		Equal		Equal	
Heating/Cooling	Refrig.	Equal		Equal		Equal	
Garage/Carport	Dbl. Gar.	Equal		Equal		Equal	
Porches, Patio, Pools, etc.	Patio/Porch Pool/Spa	Equal Pool	+1500	Equal Pool	+1500	Equal Equal	
Special Energy Efficient Items	Typical	Equal		Equal		Equal	
Fireplace(s)	None	1 Fireplace	–1500	1 Fireplace	–1500	1 Fireplace	–1500
Other (e.g. kitchen equip., remodeling)	Int. Upgrad Site Improv	Equal Equal		Equal Equal		Equal Equal	
Net Adj. (total)		+ / – $		+ / – $		+ / – $	
Indicated Value of Subject		$125,000.		$126,000.		$124,000.	

Comments on Sales Comparison: All Comparables cited are recent sales of similar or the same model as the subject. Sale 1 is felt to be most similar overall and was accorded the most weight in the final analysis. Sale 2 & 3 provide good support

INDICATED VALUE BY SALES COMPARISON APPROACH .... $ 125,000.
INDICATED VALUE BY INCOME APPROACH (If Applicable) Estimated Market Rent $ N/A /Mo. x Gross Rent Multiplier N/A = $ N/A

This appraisal is made [X] "as is" [ ] subject to the repairs, alterations, inspections or conditions listed below [ ] completion per plans and specifications.
Comments and Conditions of Appraisal: The income approach is not applicable. This report was made to estimate the fair market value.
Final Reconciliation: The market approach is most applicable. The cost approach was used as a supportive measure.

RECONCILIATION

This appraisal is based upon the above requirements, the certification, contingent and limiting conditions, and Market Value definition that are stated in
[ ] FmHA, HUD &/or VA instructions.
[X] Freddie Mac Form 439 (Rev. 7/86)/Fannie Mae Form 1004B (Rev. 7/86) filed with client _____ 19__ [ ] attached.

I (WE) ESTIMATE THE MARKET VALUE, AS DEFINED, OF THE SUBJECT PROPERTY AS OF March 30 19 88 to be $ 125,000.

I (We) certify: that to the best of my (our) knowledge and belief the facts and data used herein are true and correct; that I (we) personally inspected the subject property, both inside and out, and have made an exterior inspection of all comparable sales cited in this report; and that I (we) have no undisclosed interest, present or prospective therein.

Appraiser(s) SIGNATURE _____ NAME John D. Doe, CREA
Review Appraiser SIGNATURE _____ (if applicable) NAME _____
[ ] Did [ ] Did Not Inspect Property

Freddie Mac Form 70 10/86   Fannie Mae Form 1004 10/86

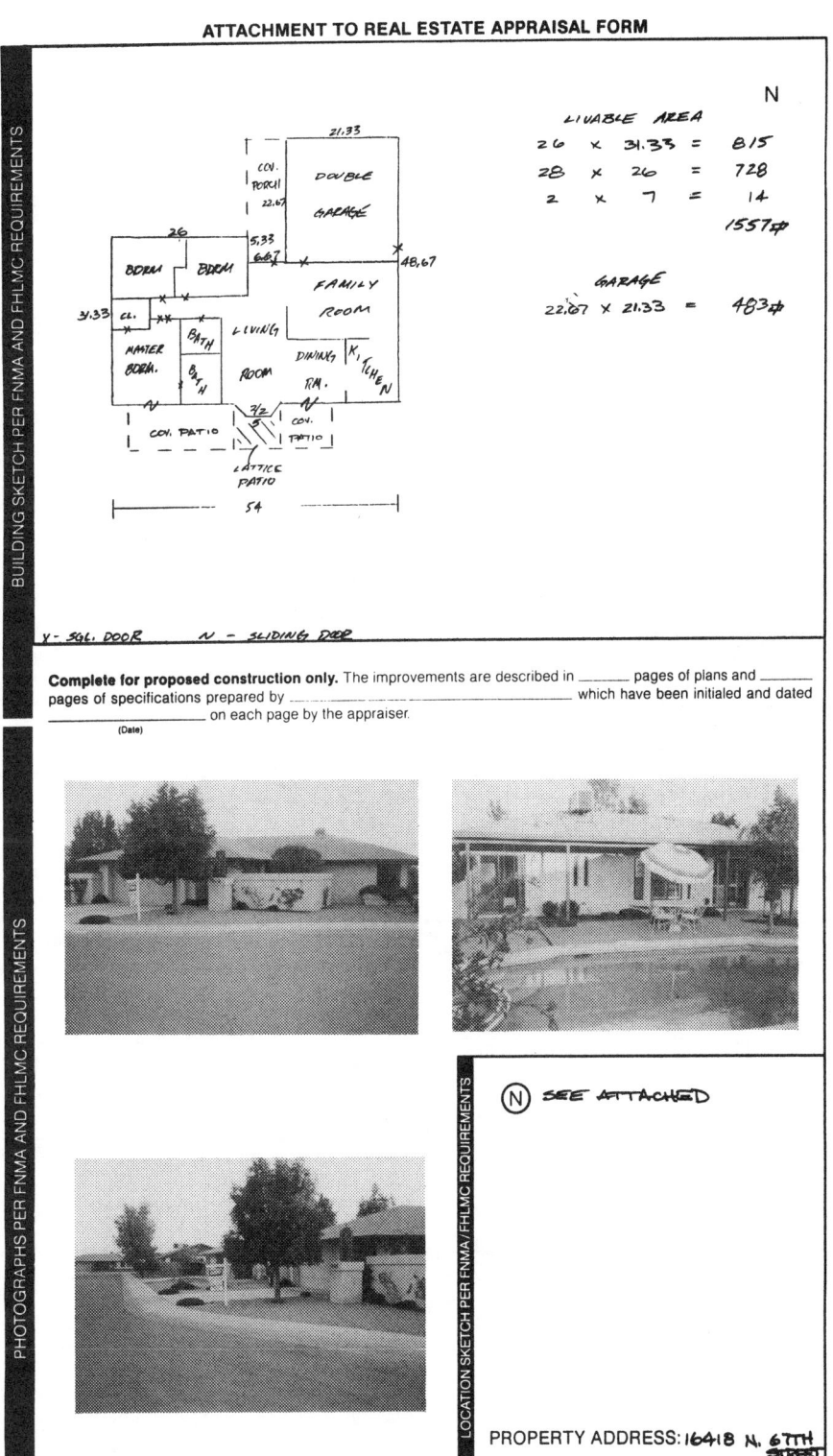

PT. NW⁴ SEC. 3 3N 4E
PT. COUNTRY TRACE: LOTS 1-18, 36-41, 52-66,
72-78, 102-104
(MCR-236-27 1982 SUB)

BOOK 215
MAP 40
SHEET 3

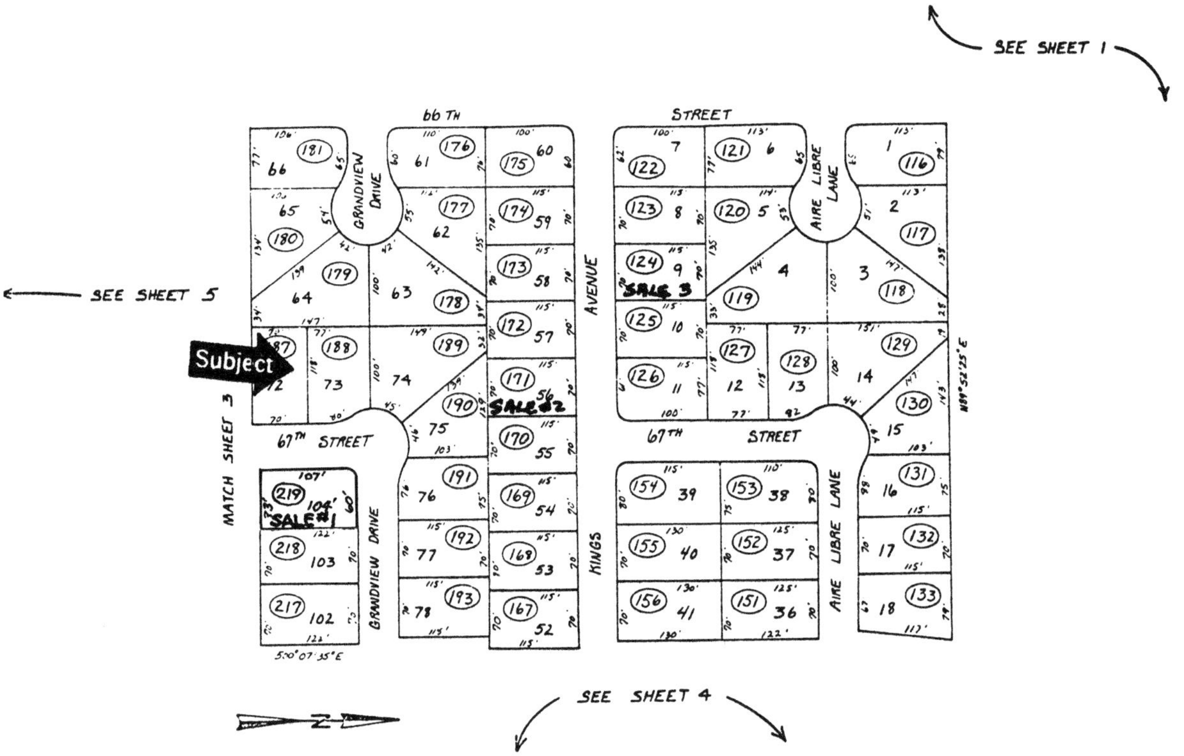

PT. NW⁴ SEC. 3 3N 4E
PT. COUNTRY TRACE: LOTS 19-35, 42-51, 79-101
(MCR 236-27 1982 SUB)

BOOK 215
MAP 40
SHEET 4

Borrower/Client **BROWN, STEPHEN L. AND MARY ANN**
Property Address **16418 N. 6TH ST.**
City **SCOTTSDALE** County **MARICOPA** State **AZ** Zip Code **85254**
Lender

COMPARABLE # 1
6707 E. GRANDVIEW

COMPARABLE # 2
6613 E. KINGS AVE

COMPARABLE # 3
6610 E KINGS AVE

ML-939 (6-85)

DEFINITION OF MARKET VALUE: The most probable price which a property should bring in a competitive and open market under all conditions requisite to a fair sale, the buyer and seller, each acting prudently, knowledgeably and assuming the price is not affected by undue stimulus. Implicit in this definition is the consummation of a sale as of a specified date and the passing of title from seller to buyer under conditions whereby: (1) buyer and seller are typically motivated; (2) both parties are well informed or well advised, and each acting in what he considers his own best interest; (3) a reasonable time is allowed for exposure in the open market; (4) payment is made in terms of cash in U.S. dollars or in terms of financial arrangements comparable thereto; and (5) the price represents the normal consideration for the property sold unaffected by special or creative financing or sales concessions* granted by anyone associated with the sale.

* Adjustments to the comparables must be made for special or creative financing or sales concessions. No adjustments are necessary for those costs which are normally paid by sellers as a result of tradition or law in a market area; these costs are readily identifiable since the seller pays these costs in virtually all sales transactions. Special or creative financing adjustments can be made to the comparable property by comparisons to financing terms offered by a third party institutional lender that is not already involved in the property or transaction. Any adjustment should not be calculated on a mechanical dollar for dollar cost of the financing or concession but the dollar amount of any adjustment should approximate the market's reaction to the financing or concessions based on the appraiser's judgment.

CERTIFICATION AND STATEMENT OF LIMITING CONDITIONS

CERTIFICATION: The Appraiser certifies and agrees that:

1. The Appraiser has no present or contemplated future interest in the property appraised; and neither the employment to make the appraisal, nor the compensation for it, is contingent upon the appraised value of the property.

2. The Appraiser has no personal interest in or bias with respect to the subject matter of the appraisal report or the participants to the sale. The "Estimate of Market Value" in the appraisal report is not based in whole or in part upon the race, color, or national origin of the prospective owners or occupants of the property appraised, or upon the race, color or national origin of the present owners or occupants of the properties in the vicinity of the property appraised.

3. The Appraiser has personally inspected the property, both inside and out, and has made an exterior inspection of all comparable sales listed in the report. To the best of the Appraiser's knowledge and belief, all statements and information in this report are true and correct, and the Appraiser has not knowingly withheld any significant information.

4. All contingent and limiting conditions are contained herein (imposed by the terms of the assignment or by the undersigned affecting the analyses, opinions, and conclusions contained in the report).

5. This appraisal report has been made in conformity with and is subject to the requirements of the Code of Professional Ethics and Standards of Professional Conduct of the appraisal organizations with which the Appraiser is affiliated.

6. All conclusions and opinions concerning the real estate that are set forth in the appraisal report were prepared by the Appraiser whose signature appears on the appraisal report, unless indicated as "Review Appraiser." No change of any item in the appraisal report shall be made by anyone other than the Appraiser, and the Appraiser shall have no responsibility for any such unauthorized change.

CONTINGENT AND LIMITING CONDITIONS: The certification of the Appraiser appearing in the appraisal report is subject to the following conditions and to such other specific and limiting conditions as are set forth by the Appraiser in the report.

1. The Appraiser assumes no responsibility for matters of a legal nature affecting the property appraised or the title thereto, nor does the Appraiser render any opinion as to the title, which is assumed to be good and marketable. The property is appraised as though under responsible ownership.

2. Any sketch in the report may show approximate dimensions and is included to assist the reader in visualizing the property. The Appraiser has made no survey of the property.

3. The Appraiser is not required to give testimony or appear in court because of having made the appraisal with reference to the property in question, unless arrangements have been previously made therefor.

4. Any distribution of the valuation in the report between land and improvements applies only under the existing program of utilization. The separate valuations for land and building must not be used in conjunction with any other appraisal and are invalid if so used.

5. The Appraiser assumes that there are no hidden or unapparent conditions of the property, subsoil, or structures, which would render it more or less valuable. The Appraiser assumes no responsibility for such conditions, or for engineering which might be required to discover such factors.

6. Information, estimates, and opinions furnished to the Appraiser, and contained in the report, were obtained from sources considered reliable and believed to be true and correct. However, no responsibility for accuracy of such items furnished the Appraiser can be assumed by the Appraiser.

7. Disclosure of the contents of the appraisal report is governed by the Bylaws and Regulations of the professional appraisal organizations with which the Appraiser is affiliated.

8. Neither all, nor any part of the content of the report, or copy thereof (including conclusions as to the property value, the identity of the Appraiser, professional designations; reference to any professional appraisal organizations, or the firm with which the Appraiser is connected), shall be used for any purposes by anyone but the client specified in the report, the borrower if appraisal fee paid by same, the mortgagee or its successors and assigns, mortgage insurers, consultants, professional appraisal organizations, any state or federally approved financial institution, any department, agency, or instrumentality of the United States or any state or the District of Columbia, without the previous written consent of the Appraiser; nor shall it be conveyed by anyone to the public through advertising, public relations, news, sales, or other media, without the written consent and approval of the Appraiser.

9. On all appraisals, subject to satisfactory completion, repairs, or alterations, the appraisal report and value conclusion are contingent upon completion of the improvements in a workmanlike manner.

Date: 3-30-88   Appraiser(s): John D Brown, CREA

FREDDIE MAC
FORM 439 JUL 86
USF 00600

U.S. Forms Inc., 2 Central Sq., Grafton, MA 01519-0446   1-800-225-9583   1-839-4417

FANNIE MAE
FORM 1004B JUL 86

VIII   Supplements

COMMON ERRORS AND DEFICIENCIES IN APPRAISAL REPORTS

by the National Association of Review Appraisers and Mortgage Underwriters

The following list of appraisal problems has been presented to direct the underwriter's attention to important appraisal considerations. An understanding of these items can help the underwriter and/or reviewer to spot poor quality appraisal reports. The common errors and deficiencies listed below are the most common problems faced by individuals whose daily task is to review residential appraisal reports.

- **Subject and comparables not located anywhere near each other.** Good comparables are recent sales of similar properties from the subject neighborhood. Frequently, appraisers use comparables that are located many miles from the subject property.
- **Comparables that are not comparable.** Frequently, comparable data is inadequate because the comparables are not even remotely similar to the subject. Poor selection of market data is one of the worst problems financial institutions experience in reviewing appraisal reports.
- **Old comparables.** Again, proper appraisal practice requires that the appraiser select recent sales of similar properties from the subject neighborhood.
- **Over-appraised properties.** Over-appraised properties are one of the chief concerns of the financial community because they increase the magnitude of our loss when a default occurs.
- **Missing or inaccurate information.** Often, appraisers leave out vital information that is important in the loan underwriting process. Many a property has been underwritten that would have been rejected if the appraisal report were accurate.
- **Failure to bracket sales data.** Appraisers should find comparables that are a little better than the subject, those that are not quite as good, as well as properties that fall between these poles. This will allow the appraiser to establish a range and allow him or her, by adjustments, to find a point within the range where the subject property can be placed.
- **Consistently listing sales price as market value.** Sales price and market value are two different concepts. Many appraisers are now backing into the market approach to value.
- **Excessive adjustments.** Large adjustments indicate that the appraiser has selected inappropriate market data. This can result in properties being over-appraised. When properties are substantially over-appraised, the companies' loss can also be substantial.
- **Using construction cost figures to indicate the subject property's "Fair Market Value".** Cost does not necessarily equal value. Attempting to justify a loan based upon construction costs is risky. Construction costs may not be supported in the marketplace.
- **Handwritten appraisal reports.** A professional appraisal report should be typed, with the appraiser's name typed under his or her signature. Handwritten reports are hard to read. Frequently, they are illegible.
- **Inconsistent adjustment patterns.** Appraisers sometimes adjust value factors in an inconsistent manner without any explanation of why similar features are given dissimilar adjustments.
- **Lack of clarity with respect to the appraiser's reasoning procedures.** An appraisal report is supposed to be a logical document that you can read, step by step, and come to the same conclusion as the appraiser.

- **Report is inadequate with respect to neighborhood data and trends.** Often, important information on the neighborhood is missing. Inadequate or missing information can lead the underwriter to make decisions that are contrary to the company's underwriting guidelines.
- **Report is too short or brief to adequately cover the property being appraised.** The appraiser should spend the time and effort necessary to adequately describe and appraise the subject property. If the form does not contain enough space to explain special property features or problems connected with the property and/or market, the appraiser should use additional pages to cover topics that cannot be adequately described on the appraisal form.
- **Positive or negative features of the property are not mentioned.** The appraiser should clarify both positive and negative features of the subject property. How can the underwriter make an intelligent decision if he or she does not know the strong or weak points associated with the subject property. Underwriting is a judgmental process. The underwriter needs to know the factors that positively or adversely affect the value and marketability of the subject property.
- **Missing photographs or photographs that do not adequately show the subject property and its surroundings.** When the underwriter's vision is limited due to poor quality photographs, so is the underwriter's judgment. The underwriter, in underwriting a loan, is trying to see. In a variety of ways, the appraiser is literally the underwriter's eyes and ears.
- **Errors in reports.** Errors may exist in the appraisal report due to faulty or missing information, as well as from inappropriate handling of market or other data.
- **Making unsupportable adjustments.** Many appraisal reports lack credibility because the appraiser's adjustments are illogical, as well as unconvincing.
- **Properties that lack marketability.** Appraisers often fail to comment on marketability. This is important, especially when there are apparent marketability problems within a given geographic area.

The underwriter's or reviewer's job with respect to appraising, is to secure acceptable appraisal reports; reports that meet standards set by professional appraisal societies. The underwriter and reviewer are the company's last defense before the loan is underwritten. Thus, the underwriter/reviewer's task is one of quality control. In reviewing appraisal reports, companies are attempting to protect themselves from an unreasonable degree of risk. Financial institutions should expect to take risks. However, the risks should be normal.

Common Appraisal Deficiencies Identified by HUD Review Appraisers

Selection and Analysis of Comparable Properties

- **Not Using Conventional Sales.** HUD requires that each appraisal include at least one conventional comparable. Even in areas where the conventional market is limited, every attempt should be made to locate conventional sales. Appraisers are not restricted to sales in the immediate neighborhood of the property being appraised.

- **Using Outdated Sales Data.** HUD requirements stress the need to use current sales data. Value is derived from recent sales of similar properties. In metropolitan areas, HUD uses a 6-month limitation. Using recent sales is particularly important in areas where market values are declining.

- **Selecting Poor Sales Data.** Properties selected for comparison should furnish accommodations, livability, and amenities within a range of similarity to the property being appraised. Examples of comparables that are not sufficiently similar include using comparables: (a) that are significantly different in size from the appraised property (e.g., square footage of comparables that are 20 to 50 percent different than subject property); (b) with significant age variances (e.g., using comparables that are 20, 30, etc., years older than property being appraised); and (c) with room variances (e.g., two 1-bedroom and one 4-bedroom comparables would not be comparable to a 2-bedroom property). When properties are not sufficiently similar, excessive adjustments are required. When this occurs, it is not known if the appraiser's estimate of value is indicative of the market value of other similar properties.

- **Not Bracketing Sales.** In selecting properties for comparison, it is desirable to choose some that are equivalent (i.e., provide equal accommodations, such as the same number of square feet) and some that are nearly equivalent to the property being appraised. Nearly equivalent properties should include some better than and some not as good as the property in order that comparisons can be made within the established bracket.

- **Making Inadequate Adjustments to Comparables.** Appropriate adjustments must be made for differences in age, special types of financial arrangements, amenities, lot size, etc. Adjustments are to be made from interpolation of selected market data. For example, comparable A does not have a garage and sold for $50,000. Comparable B is similar to A and has a garage, as does the property being appraised, and it sold for $51,500. Thus the adjustment would be $1,500 for a garage regardless of the cost of new construction.

- **Constantly Listing Sales Price as Market Value.** Sales price and market value are different concepts. Although they can be the same, they usually are not. When comparables are adjusted with the intent of raising the appraised value to get to the sales price figure, the basic purpose of the appraisal process is negated. All of the individuals involved in the appraisal process (the buyer, seller, lender, and real estate broker) have a financial interest in the processing and sale of a home under consideration for HUD mortgage insurance. There may be times when the appraiser is under pressure from these individuals to have appraisals "come in" at or over the sales price. Although these pressures may exist, the appraiser should remember that his/her ultimate responsibility is to ensure that HUD is underwriting a sound structure at a reasonable value, thus limiting the risk to the FHA insurance fund. In situations where undue pressure is exerted, it may be appropriate to turn down appraisal assignments.

Examples of Unacceptable Appraisal Practices
by the Federal National Mortgage Association

The following are examples of appraisal practices that Fannie Mae consider as unacceptable:

- Inclusion of inaccurate factual data about the subject neighborhood, site, improvements, or comparable sales;
- Failure to comment on negative factors with respect to the subject neighborhood, subject property, or proximity of the subject property to adverse influences;

- Use of comparables in the valuation process even though the appraiser has not personally inspected the exterior of the comparables by, at least, driving by them;
- Selection and use of inappropriate comparable sales or the failure to use comparables that are locationally and physically the most similar to the subject property;
- Use of data—particularly comparable sales data—that was provided by parties who have a financial interest in the sale or financing of the subject property without the appraiser's verification of the information from a disinterested source. For example, it would be inappropriate for an appraiser to use comparable sales provided by the real estate broker who is handling the sale of the subject property, unless the appraiser verifies the accuracy of the data provided with another source and makes an independent investigation to determine that the comparables provided were the best ones available;
- Use of adjustments to the comparable sales that do not reflect the market's reaction to the differences between the subject property and the comparables, or the failure to make adjustments when they are clearly indicated;
- Development of a valuation conclusion that is based—either partially or completely—on the race, color, or national origin of either the prospective owners or occupants of the subject property or of the present owners or occupants of the properties in the vicinity of the subject property; and
- Development of a valuation conclusion that is not supported by available market data.

APPRAISAL GUIDELINES

This handout includes the following chapters from the Fannie Mae Selling Guide Updates that were published October 26, 1987. They became effective January 4, 1988 for all appraisals completed on or after that date. This handout includes the same information that was provided to all Fannie Mae approved lenders. Please note that the asteriks (***) along the right margin of each page indicates that the information on that line has been changed or is new.

1. Chapter 1 - Required Documentation
   Pages 4 - 6

2. Chapter 3 - Investment Properties
   Pages 33 - 34

3. Chapter 4 - Property and Appraisal Analysis
   Pages 35 - 66

4. Chapter 5 - Special Considerations
   Pages 67 - 77

Fannie Mae will publish a separate booklet, for the appraiser, that will contain all of the information outlined in the above chapters plus the forthcoming Fannie Mae guidelines regarding d-PUD properties. This booklet should be available during the first quarter of 1988 from any Fannie Mae approved lender.

Underwriting Guidelines

Required Documentation

Section 102

Selling

**Section 102
Standard Appraisal
Documents**

The property must have been appraised within the 12 months that precede the date of the note and mortgage. When the appraisal report will be more than four months old on the date of the note and mortgage, the original appraiser must inspect the exterior of the property and review current market data to determine that the property has not declined in value since the date of the original appraisal. We require the original appraiser to provide a certification to that effect, based on his or her exterior inspection of the property and knowledge of current market conditions. The inspection and the certification must occur within the four months that precede the date of the note and mortgage. If the appraiser cannot make the required certification, we require a new appraisal for the property.

For proposed construction, the appraisal may be based on plans and specifications if the lender obtains a certification of completion and value before it delivers the mortgage to us. This certification should be completed by the original appraiser and must be accompanied by photographs of the completed improvements. The appraiser must certify that the improvements were completed in accordance with the requirements and conditions stated in the original appraisal report and that—taking into consideration the current market conditions—the property has not declined in value since the date it was originally appraised as proposed construction. Minor items that do not affect livability may be incomplete as long as the lender has arranged for an adequate escrow to guarantee their completion. (We consider funds equal to at least one and one-half times the cost to complete the items as a reasonable amount to escrow.)

For existing construction, the improvements must be complete when the mortgage is sold to us. The appraisal may be based on the "as is" condition of the property if minor conditions that do not affect the livability of the property exist—such as minor peeling paint or minor deferred maintenance—as long as the appraiser's estimate of value reflects the existence of these conditions. The lender must review carefully the appraisal for a property appraised in an "as is" condition to assure that the property does not have any physical deficiencies or conditions that would affect its livability. If there are none, the lender does not need to require minor repairs to be completed before it sells the mortgage to us. When there are incomplete items or conditions that do affect the livability of the property—such as a partially completed addition or renovation—or physical deficiencies that could affect the soundness or structural integrity of the improvements, the property must be appraised subject to completion of the specific alterations or repairs. In such cases, the lender must obtain a certificate of completion before it delivers the mortgage to us. The certification must be completed by the original appraiser.

Selling

Underwriting Guidelines

Required Documentation

Section 102

The certification does not need to include photographs of the property unless those that accompanied the original appraisal report are no longer representative of the completed property.

If the original appraiser is not available to complete a certification of completion or value when we require it, the lender may use a substitute appraiser as long as it explains why the original appraiser was not used. The substitute appraiser must review the original appraisal and certify that the appraiser's estimate of market value was reasonable on the date of the original appraisal report.

Our appraisal report forms are designed to provide a concise format for presenting the appraiser's description and valuation. The appraiser must complete these forms in a way that will clearly reflect the results of his or her thorough investigation and analysis and provide the rationale for the estimate of market value. The appraisal report that should be used depends on the type of property that is being appraised. The appraiser must use the latest version of one of the following forms:

- *Uniform Residential Appraisal Report* (Form 1004) for single-family properties, including *de minimis* PUD units;

- *Appraisal Report - Small Residential Income Property* (Form 1025) for two- to four-family properties; or

- *Appraisal Report - Individual Condominium or PUD Unit* (Form 1073) for properties that are units in condominium, PUD, and cooperative projects.

We also require certain exhibits to support each appraisal report:

a. A *Certification and Statement of Limiting Conditions* (Form 1004B), when one is not already on file with the lender. (If the appraiser makes an addition or deletion to this certification, he or she must reference the change in the "reconciliation" section of the appraisal report. Since we will not purchase a mortgage if the appraiser's changes to Form 1004B alter the definition of market value or conflict with any of our property and appraisal analysis underwriting guidelines, the lender should review carefully any changes that were made.);

b. A street map that shows the location of the subject property and of all comparables that the appraiser used;

Underwriting Guidelines

Required Documentation

Section 103 # Selling

c. An exterior building sketch of the improvements that indicates the dimensions. A floor plan sketch is not required unless the floor plan is functionally obsolete, resulting in a limited market appeal for the property in comparison to competitive properties in the neighborhood. For units in condominium or cooperative projects, interior perimeter unit dimensions are required instead of exterior building dimensions;

d. Clear, descriptive photographs that show the front, back, and a street scene of the subject property, and that are appropriately identified by the property address;

e. Clear, descriptive photographs that show the front of each comparable property and that are appropriately identified by the property address. Generally, these photographs should be originals; however, copies of photographs from a multiple listing service, or copies of photographs from the appraiser's files, are acceptable if they are clear and descriptive;

f. Certification of Completion and Value—either as a letter or as a form that provides the necessary information—if applicable;

g. An *Operating Income Statement* (Form 216), which has been jointly prepared by the applicant, the lender, and the appraiser, and which includes the appraiser's comments on the reasonableness of the projected operating income, if the property is an investment property;

h. A *Single-Family Comparable Rent Schedule* (Form 1007) for single-family investment properties; and

i. Any other data—as an attachment or addendum to the appraisal report form—that are necessary to provide an adequately supported estimate of market value.

**Section 103
TimeSaver
Documentation**

The TimeSaver Documentation alternative allows lenders to obtain documentation related to a borrower's income, employment, funds for closing, and mortgage payment history directly from the borrower, rather than from the borrower's employer, bank, or mortgage servicer. TimeSaver Documentation may not meet the needs of every borrower and every lender. For example, the different formats and information provided by the various types of substitute documents may require more analysis and judgment on the part of the lender's processors and underwriters, even though the overall processing time is reduced. We rely on lenders to use their good judgment in determining when this substitute documentation alternative would be appropriate for their customers and internal operations.

Underwriting Guidelines
Property and Appraisal Analysis

Selling

Chapter 4. Property and Appraisal Analysis

This Chapter details our general requirements for underwriting the property/appraisal aspects of mortgages made on one- to four-family properties. (Certain types of housing—cooperative units; energy-efficient properties; manufactured housing (or factory-built) units; condominum, PUD and *de minimis* PUD units; mixed-use properties; and properties affected by environmental hazards or substances—merit special consideration in the appraisal review, so we discuss specific requirements for them in Chapter 5.) Because the evaluation of a property is such a vital part of the risk analysis, we expect lenders to place as much emphasis on underwriting the property and reviewing the appraisal as they do on underwriting the borrower's creditworthiness.

Because Fannie Mae holds the lender responsible for the accuracy of the appraisal, it is important for underwriters to understand their role in the appraisal process and their relationship to the appraiser.

- The underwriter's role is to analyze the property based on the appraisal and to judge the property's acceptability as security for the mortgage requested.

- The appraiser's role is to provide the lender with an adequately supported estimate of value and a complete, accurate description of the property.

When the information or methodology of an appraisal requires additional clarification or justification, the underwriter must obtain from the appraiser any information that is necessary to make an informed decision concerning the property. Because it is essential for the lender to have an independent, disinterested examination and valuation of the property, the lender must order the appraisal report, rather than allowing the borrower to do so. The appraiser must remain free of any outside influence in the valuation process. This is at the heart of a good underwriting system. We require appraisers to provide complete and accurate reports. The estimate of market value must represent the appraiser's professional conclusion, based on market data, logical analysis, and judgment.

These requirements are intended to provide guidance to underwriters and appraisers as to the type of information that is needed to make a prudent underwriting decision. They are also designed to provide what we feel are minimum acceptable appraisal standards. We recognize that the appraiser's analysis may not comply with our specific guidelines for every appraisal problem. We allow the appraiser discretion to properly develop the value estimate. The appraiser must, however, provide sound reasoning in his or her appraisal report for working outside of our standards.

Underwriting Guidelines
Property and Appraisal Analysis

Section 401.01

Selling

**Section 401
Appraiser Qualifications**

Fannie Mae does not approve appraisers. Therefore, lenders must not give any consideration to an appraiser's representation that he or she is approved or qualified by Fannie Mae. Lenders are responsible for the selection of appraisers and will be solely accountable for their performance. Lenders must take appropriate steps to ensure that an appraiser is qualified to perform appraisals for the particular types of property that the lender intends to refer to that appraiser.

We recognize that, in some instances, a lender will approve an appraiser subject to the appraiser's work being reviewed and signed by a review appraiser—typically, the review appraiser is the appraiser's employer or supervisor, who is also assuming full responsibility for the quality of the appraisal. When a given appraiser or appraisal service uses review appraisers, the lender should review the qualifications of both the appraiser and the review appraiser, and should not rely solely on the qualifications of the review appraiser. Since we consider the appraiser to be the individual who personally inspected the subject property; inspected the exterior of the comparables; performed the analysis; and prepared, certified, and signed the report as the appraiser, we do not require review appraisers to sign appraisal reports. However, when a review appraiser signs the appraisal, that individual is indicating his or her concurrence with the contents of the appraisal report. In addition, the review appraiser must indicate on the appraisal report form whether he or she personally inspected both the inside and the outside of the subject property.

Fannie Mae has the right, at any time, to refuse to accept appraisals prepared by specific appraisers or to notify a lender that we will no longer accept appraisals prepared by a given appraiser. When we notify a lender that this is the case, we will allow the lender a certain amount of time to clear its mortgage pipeline—after that, it must not submit to us mortgages secured by any properties that were appraised by that individual.

**Section 401.01
Review of Qualifications**

When evaluating an appraiser's qualifications, a lender should review the appraiser's education and experience, sample appraisals, professional affiliations, and references from prior clients and employers. The appraiser must be experienced in appraising the types of properties that the lender intends to use his or her services for, and should currently be active in appraisal work. Before using an appraiser's services, the lender should be satisfied that the appraiser has demonstrated the ability to perform quality appraisals. For this reason, lenders should review actual samples of an appraiser's work to assure that the appraiser does not employ any of the appraisal practices that we list in Section 402.02 as unacceptable practices.

Selling

Underwriting Guidelines
Property and Appraisal Analysis

Section 402.01

While we do not require professional appraisal designations, they can be helpful to lenders in evaluating an appraiser's qualifications, particularly when the designation is from a nationally recognized organization that has formal experience, education and ethics requirements that are strongly administered. If the lender considers an appraisal designation in its evaluation, it should be familiar with the appraisal organization's specific requirements to assure that the designation is evaluated appropriately.

**Section 401.02
On-going Review of Appraisals**

Lenders must continually evaluate the quality of the appraiser's work through the normal underwriting review of all appraisal reports, as well as through the spot-check field review of appraisals as part of its Quality Control System. Lenders must be satisfied that any appraisers they use for spot-check field reviews are well-qualified.

**Section 402
Reviewing the Appraisal Report**

Fannie Mae holds the lender responsible for the quality of the appraisal it uses to support the market value of a security property. Therefore, the lender must make sure that it not only provides the appraiser with appropriate information about the financing and sales data, but also that it has sufficient knowledge of our appraisal requirements to enable it to determine that the appraiser has properly addressed our specific criteria and that the appraiser has not engaged in any unacceptable appraisal practices.

The remainder of this Chapter is presented in the general order that the major topics appear in on the *Uniform Residential Appraisal Report* (Form 1004), thus providing lenders with a usable working reference that can be applied generally to all of our different appraisal report forms. The appraiser is responsible for completing Form 1004 in its entirety, except for the "Lender Discretionary Use" box that is located in the upper right-hand corner of the form.

**Section 402.01
Lender-supplied Information**

The lender must tell the appraiser about all financing data and sales concessions for the property that will be, or have been, granted by anyone associated with the transaction. Generally, this can be accomplished by providing the appraiser a copy of the complete, ratified sales contract for the property that is to be appraised. If the lender is aware of additional pertinent information that is not included in the sales contract, it should inform the appraiser. Information that must be disclosed includes:

- settlement charges;
- loan fees or charges;

Underwriting Guidelines
Property and Appraisal Analysis

Section 402.02

Selling

- discounts to the sales price;
- payment of condominum/PUD fees;
- interest rate buydowns, or other below-market-rate financing;
- credits or refunds of the borrower's expenses;
- absorption of monthly payments;
- assignment of rent payments; and
- non-realty items that were included in the transaction.

The upper right-hand corner of the *Uniform Residential Appraisal Report* (Form 1004) contains a box titled "Lender Discretionary Use", which is included to encourage lenders to provide closing data to comparable sales reporting services. We do not require lenders to complete this section of Form 1004, but, if the lender does complete it, the lender should provide the specific contract information after the closing or loan settlement.

Section 402.02 Unacceptable Appraisal Practices

The following are examples of appraisal practices that we consider as unacceptable:

- Inclusion of inaccurate factual data about the subject neighborhood, site, improvements, or comparable sales;

- Failure to comment on negative factors with respect to the subject neighborhood, subject property, or proximity of the subject property to adverse influences;

- Use of comparables in the valuation process even though the appraiser has not personally inspected the exterior of the comparables by, at least, driving by them;

- Selection and use of inappropriate comparable sales or the failure to use comparables that are locationally and physically the most similar to the subject property;

- Use of data—particularly comparable sales data—that was provided by parties who have a financial interest in the sale or financing of the subject property without the appraiser's verification of the information from a disinterested source. For example, it would be inappropriate for an appraiser to use comparable sales provided by the real estate broker who is handling the sale of the subject property, unless the appraiser verifies the accuracy of the data provided with another source and makes an independent investigation to determine that the comparables provided were the best ones available;

- Use of adjustments to the comparable sales that do not reflect the market's reaction to the differences between the subject prop-

Underwriting Guidelines
Property and Appraisal Analysis

Selling

Section 403

erty and the comparables, or the failure to make adjustments when they are clearly indicated;

- Development of a valuation conclusion that is based—either partially or completely—on the race, color, or national origin of either the prospective owners or occupants of the subject property or of the present owners or occupants of the properties in the vicinity of the subject property; and

- Development of a valuation conclusion that is not supported by available market data.

**Section 403
The Subject Property**

The first section of the *Uniform Residential Appraisal Report* (Form 1004) is used to identify the subject property, to describe the property rights to be appraised, and to summarize financing data and sales concessions.

The appraiser must identify the subject property by its complete property address and legal description; a post office box number is not acceptable. The appraiser should indicate the nearest intersection if a house number is not available. When the legal description is lengthy, the appraiser may attach the full description as an addendum to the appraisal report, or may refer simply to its location in the public records.

(also see Sections 501 and 508)

The appraiser must identify the property rights to be appraised as "fee simple" or "leasehold". In addition, the appraiser must indicate whether the subject property is located in a PUD, *de minimis* PUD, condominum, or cooperative project. [Note: The appraisal for units in PUD, condominium, or cooperative projects must be completed on an *Appraisal Report—Individual Condominum or PUD Unit* (Form 1073).]

The appraiser must state the total dollar amount of the loan charges and/or concessions that will be paid by the seller (or any other party who has a financial interest in the sale or financing of the subject property) and provide a brief description of the items on the appraisal report form. If the appraiser knows that the appraisal will be used for a refinance transaction, he or she should indicate that on the form.

If the appraiser is completing one of our appraisal report forms that uses the phrase "To be completed by lender" to identify the top portion of the form—the *Appraisal Report-Small Residential Income Property* (Form 1025), the *Appraisal Report-Individual Condominium or PUD Unit* (Form 1073), or the *Loan Valuation Summary for Second Mortgages* (Form 219)—the appraiser must complete any information that the lender does not provide, including the above information related to the financing terms. If the lender did not provide a copy of the sales contract and the appraiser is not aware of

Underwriting Guidelines
Property and Appraisal Analysis

Section 404

Selling

the financing terms, he or she should include a statement to that effect.

**Section 404
Neighborhood Analysis**

The purpose of a neighborhood analysis is to identify the area—based on common characteristics or trends—that is subject to the same influences as the subject property. The sales prices of comparable properties in the identified area should reflect the positive and negative influences of the neighborhood.

A neighborhood analysis should consider the influence of social, economic, government, and environmental forces on property values in the subject neighborhood. However, neither the racial composition nor the age of a neighborhood is a reliable appraisal factor. A property located in an older neighborhood can be as sound an investment as a property located in a new neighborhood, and a property located in a neighborhood inhabited primarily by members of one race can be as sound an investment as one located in a racially mixed neighborhood or in a neighborhood inhabited primarily by a different race. The appraiser must be impartial and specific in describing favorable or unfavorable factors in a neighborhood, and should avoid the use of subjective terms or phrases such as "pride of ownership", etc.

Fannie Mae does not designate certain areas as being acceptable or unacceptable—in other words, Fannie Mae does not "red-line". Locational factors are fundamental to proper appraising and prudent underwriting, and there is nothing improper about underwriting on the basis of a realistic perception of risk in a given neighborhood. Redlining can occur when perceived property risks are based on improper locational factors—such as the arbitrary granting of unfavorable loan terms on the basis of geographic area—or when the perceptions of risk are derived from factors that do not predict risk—either reliably or not at all. An example of a factor that is not predictive of risk is race—and racial redlining is illegal under Federal law. Other factors that serve as a proxy for race are equally impermissible. The appraiser, and the lender's underwriter, must be sensitive to these impermissible factors and apply Fannie Mae's guidelines in a consistent, equitable manner. None of our property guidelines is intended to foster redlining—if any provision is interpreted to do so, it has been misunderstood.

The appraiser should explain any changes that have occurred that might influence the marketability of the properties within the neighborhood. The appraiser also must comment if there is market resistance to a neighborhood because of the known presence of an environmental hazard or any other factor. The lender must be satisfied that the neighborhood will be acceptable to a sufficient number of buyers to support an active, on-going market for the property.

Selling

Underwriting Guidelines
Property and Appraisal Analysis

Section 404.01

Some lenders underwrite loans in urban areas on a block-by-block basis. Block-by-block underwriting and appraisal analysis are acceptable in cases in which rehabilitation has started—either in the block where the subject property is located or in facing blocks visible to the property—but has not yet spread to the rest of the neighborhood. The acceptability of this type of appraising or underwriting is conditioned on the appraiser demonstrating that local conditions make it appropriate and that all essential factors are considered.

Our appraisal report forms require the appraiser to address several important factors that are used to analyze the neighborhood's impact on the property's marketability. Some of the key factors are discussed in the following subsections.

Section 404.01 Location

We will purchase mortgages that are secured by residential properties in urban, suburban, or rural areas. An "urban" location relates to a city, a "suburban" location relates to the area adjacent to a city, and a "rural" location relates to the country or anything beyond the suburban area. We do not designate certain areas as being acceptable or unacceptable.

To be eligible for purchase by Fannie Mae, a mortgage must be secured by a property that is residential in nature—based on the description of the subject property, zoning, and the present land use. We do not purchase mortgages on agricultural-type properties (such as farms, orchards, or ranches), on undeveloped land, or on land development-type properties.

Lenders must give properties with outbuildings special consideration in their underwriting and appraisal review. Properties with minimal outbuildings—such as a small barn or stable—that are of relatively insignificant value in relation to the total appraised value of the subject property are acceptable if they are typical residential improvements and support the residential use for the location and property type. For example, a property that has a small barn or stable is acceptable if the appraiser demonstrates through the use of comparable sales with similar improvements that the improvements are typical residential improvements for which an active, viable residential market exists. If the outbuildings do not represent typical residential improvements for the location and property type, the typical purchaser in the market would probably recognize minimal, if any, contributory value for them. A property with an atypical minimal outbuilding is acceptable to Fannie Mae, as long as the appraiser's analysis reflects little (or no) contributory value for it.

On the other hand, properties with significant outbuildings—such as a large barn, a storage area or facilities for farm-type animals, or a silo—must be reviewed with great care, regardless of whether the appraiser assigns any value to the outbuildings because their

Underwriting Guidelines
Property and Appraisal Analysis

Section 404.02

Selling

existence will probably indicate that the property is agricultural in nature.

All properties must be readily accessible by roads that meet local standards, and must have adequate utilities available and in service. The appraiser must also consider the present or anticipated use of any adjoining property that may adversely affect the value or marketability of the subject property.

Certain aspects of the location of a property will require special consideration. For example, properties in resort areas that attract people for seasonal or vacation use are acceptable only if they are suitable for year-round use. Any property that is not suitable for year-round occupancy—regardless of where it is located—is unacceptable.

Section 404.02
Degree of Development and Growth Rate

The degree of development of a neighborhood (which is referred to as "built-up" on the appraisal report forms) is the percentage of the available land in the neighborhood that has been improved. Areas that are less than 25% developed are not acceptable for maximum financing. Areas that are between 25% and 75% developed are suitable for maximum financing if they show at least a stable or steady growth rate. Areas that are more than 75% developed, are viable, and are not experiencing declining property values are acceptable for maximum financing.

An area's degree of development may indicate whether a particular property is residential in nature. Generally, we will not purchase a mortgage that is secured by a property in a rural area or any other area that is less than 25% developed if the value of the site exceeds 30% of the total appraised value of the security property. However, if this higher site value is typical in the area (and market acceptance can be demonstrated through the use of comparable properties), we will purchase the mortgage. For example, if the typical single-family building site in a particular area—based on the zoning, the highest and best use of the land, and the present land use—is two acres in size, the mortgage will be eligible for purchase even if the site's value exceeds 30% of the property's total appraised value, as long as the appraiser demonstrates through the use of comparable sales that the property is a typical residential property for that particular neighborhood.

Because we do not purchase mortgages secured by agricultural-type properties, undeveloped land, or land-development-type properties, the lender must review carefully the appraisal report for properties that have sites larger than those typical for residential properties in the area. Special attention must be given to the appraiser's description of the neighborhood, zoning, the highest and best use determination, and the degree of comparability between the subject property and the comparable sales. If the subject property has a

	Underwriting Guidelines
	Property and Appraisal Analysis
Selling	Section 404.05

	significantly larger site than the comparables used in the appraiser's analysis, the subject property may not be a typical residential property for the neighborhood.
Section 404.03 Property Values	Maximum financing is acceptable when property values are stable or increasing. If values are declining, the appraiser should comment on the reason for the decline and its effect on the property's marketability. Properties in such areas must be reviewed with great care. The reasons for a decline in values and the probability of its continuance are key considerations in the property's acceptability. The lender must not consider the use of maximum financing in any instance in which property values are declining.
Section 404.04 Demand/Supply and Marketing Time	An over-supply of housing is not desirable, since it indicates that properties are selling slowly with a lot of competition. A shortage of properties or a balanced situation is preferred. An over-supply of properties may be a neighborhood-wide or a city-wide problem. In either case, the appraiser must comment on the reason for the over-supply and its effect on the property's value.
	Marketing time is the average time that it takes for a reasonably priced property to sell in the subject neighborhood. When marketing time for a particular area is greater than six months, the appraiser must comment on the reason for the extended marketing period and its effect on the property's value.
Section 404.05 Present Land Use	Typically, dwellings best maintain their value when they are situated in neighborhoods that consist of other similar dwellings. Therefore, a single-family property in a neighborhood with apartments and commercial or industrial development may not have the stability required to sustain value over a long period of time. However, the negative impression of a property within a mixed-use neighborhood can be offset by factors that enhance the market value of the property through increased buyer demand. Typical factors include such things as easy access to employment centers and a high level of community activity. Viable older neighborhoods frequently reflect a successful mixing of commercial service uses—such as grocery and other neighborhood stores or occasional multifamily properties.
	The appraiser should provide the relative percentages of the developed land in the neighborhood in the "Present Land Use" section of the appraisal report form, rather than simply referring to the zoning classifications. The appraiser should report separately the percentage of developed single-family sites, developed two- to four-family sites, etc. Undeveloped land should be reported as vacant. In addition, if there is a significant amount of vacant or undeveloped land in the neighborhood, the appraiser should include comments to

Underwriting Guidelines
Property and Appraisal Analysis

Section 404.07

Selling

that effect in the "Neighborhood Comments" section of the report to assure that he or she adequately describes the neighborhood. If the present land use in the neighborhood is not one of those listed on the appraisal report form—such as parkland—the appraiser must also indicate in the "Neighborhood Comments" section the type of land use and its related percentage. The total of the types of land uses must equal 100%.

Section 404.06
Changes in Land Use

Fannie Mae relies on the present land use, the predominant occupancy composition, and the likelihood that either will change to determine whether a neighborhood is undergoing transition. A "neighborhood in transition" description must not be used to refer to the racial or ethnic composition—or the prospective racial or ethnic composition—of a neighborhood.

The use of maximum financing must be carefully considered when the appraiser has indicated that an area is undergoing transition that could have a negative impact on property value. For example, a neighborhood that is changing from a single-family use to a two- to four-family residential use could experience a negative effect on the marketability and values of properties in the neighborhood.

Properties also may change from owner-occupied to tenant-occupied, which can result in deterioration in the general appearance of the property and a consequent loss in value. Owner-occupancy contributes greatly to the likelihood of long-term sustained value, since owners generally find it in their best interests to maintain their property. While many tenants take excellent care of property, deterioration can occur. A high vacancy rate in the neighborhood must also be considered in terms of its long-range effect.

Section 404.07
Price Range and Predominant Price

The appraiser must indicate the price range and predominant price of properties in the subject neighborhood. The price range must reflect high and low prevailing prices of single-family residential properties—however, isolated high and low extremes should be excluded from the range. The predominant price is that which is the most common or most frequently found in the neighborhood. The appraiser may state the predominant price as a single figure or as a range (if that is more appropriate).

When the subject property has a sales price (or value) that exceeds the upper price range, the property is considered as an "over-improvement" for the neighborhood. The property is considered as an "under-improvement" if its sales price (or value) is less than the lower price range. If the subject property is an over-improvement, the loan terms generally should be more conservative because the property may not be acceptable to typical purchasers. The appraiser must explain why the property is an over- or under-improvement and comment on the adjustments that were made in the "sales comparison analysis" adjustment grid to reflect that condition.

Selling

Underwriting Guidelines
Property and Appraisal Analysis

Section 404.09

The lender should consider whether a property in an urban area is among those being renovated. Since demand for this type of property can be strong, the property should not be regarded as over-improved if there is a strong market interest, which is indicated by the existence of comparable properties.

**Section 404.08
Age Range and Predominant Age
(also see Section 408.02)**

The appraiser must indicate the age range and predominant age of properties in the subject neighborhood. The age range should reflect the oldest and newest ages of single-family residential properties—however, isolated high and low extremes should be excluded from the range. The predominant age is the one that is the most common or most frequently found in the neighborhood. The appraiser may state the predominant age as a single figure or as a range (when that is more appropriate). The appraiser should select independently the properties that he or she uses to represent the age range and predominant age, rather than merely relying on the same properties he or she used to illustrate the price range and predominant price.

The age of a property should be within the general age range of the neighborhood. Normally, neighborhoods are developed over a relatively narrow span of time so that most dwelling units will fall within a particular age range. A property that has an age outside of the general age range must receive special consideration. Unless there is strong evidence of long-term neighborhood stability, a new dwelling in an old neighborhood will carry some marginal risk. Conversely, an old dwelling in a newly developed area is generally acceptable if renovation will result in its conforming with the neighborhood.

Older properties in neighborhoods in which the improvements have been maintained in a way that sustains the properties' values are acceptable for maximum financing. Because of their location, these properties frequently will have enough advantages over newer properties in outlying areas to create equal or greater market demand. Certain older properties also may be in demand because of their unique architectural design or other factors.

**Section 404.09
Neighborhood Analysis Rating**

Our appraisal report forms provide neighborhood ratings that are designed to summarize principal items in a neighborhood that generally are considered important by purchasers when they select a home. If any rating is less-than-"average," the appraiser must comment on the reasons for the rating and its effect on the property's marketability and value. Maximum financing should not be offered to a borrower unless the property is in a location with at least "average" overall neighborhood amenities, public services, and property conditions. The appraiser should also explain any changes, either favorable or unfavorable, that have occurred (or are currently

Underwriting Guidelines
Property and Appraisal Analysis

Section 404.09

Selling

underway) if they will affect the marketability of the properties within the neighborhood. There should be sufficent market demand for the neighborhood to support an active market for the subject property.

Two items of particular importance in determining whether a neighborhood will support an active market are discussed below:

A. General appearance. The general appearance of the properties in the neighborhood is a key factor. The appraiser must consider the extent to which the properties are receiving proper maintenance. Signs of maintenance and care usually reflect a strong neighborhood with stable or increasing values.

B. Appeal to market. Essentially, this is a summary rating of the extent to which all aspects of the neighborhood will appeal to the typical purchaser in the market. An individual property by itself cannot overcome a generally prevailing reluctance of the market to invest in a neighborhood. On the other hand, a relatively weak property in a strong, viable neighborhood is likely to sustain its value, although it still must be carefully analyzed.

The appraiser must rate the various aspects of a neighborhood by comparing the characteristics for the subject neighborhood to those for competing neighborhoods. The appraiser must use the following ratings:

- *Good*, to indicate that the characteristics of the subject neighborhood are outstanding and superior to those found in competing neighborhoods;

- *Average*, to indicate that the characteristics of the subject neighborhood are equal to those that represent the "norm" for that market area and that are considered acceptable in competing neighborhoods;

- *Fair*, to indicate that the characteristics of the subject neighborhood are inferior to those that are considered acceptable in competing neighborhoods; and

- *Poor*, to indicate that the characteristics of the subject neighborhood are substantially inferior to—or in such small supply when compared to—those found in competing neighborhoods to the point that single-family residential property values are (or may be) affected adversely.

A rating of "none" or "non-existent" is not acceptable. For instance, if the subject property is in a rural location, and the norm for that location and the competing neighborhoods is that there is no public transportation, the appraiser should report the adequacy of public transportation as "average" since that is typical of competing neighborhoods.

	Underwriting Guidelines
	Property and Appraisal Analysis
Selling	Section 405.02

The appraiser must report neighborhood conditions in factual, specific terms. The use of the ratings described above does not preclude the appraiser's reporting of typical, detrimental neighborhood conditions that affect the value or marketability of the subject property. For example, if the neighborhood is characterized by a lack of maintenance or the absence of local government services (which also might be typical for competing neighborhoods), the appraiser should include a comment to that effect to provide an adequate description of the neighborhood in his or her analysis.

Section 405
Site Analysis

In order for a property to qualify for maximum financing, the site should be of a size, shape, and topography that is generally conforming and acceptable in the market area. It must also have competitive utilities, street improvements, and other amenities. Since amenities, easements, and encroachments may either detract from or enhance the site's marketability, the appraiser must comment on them if the site is not typical for the neighborhood.

Section 405.01
Zoning

The appraiser is responsible for reporting the specific zoning classification for the subject property. The appraiser must include a general statement to describe what the zoning permits—"single-family," "two-family," etc.—when he or she indicates a specific zoning such as R-1, R-2, etc. The appraiser must also include a specific statement if the improvements do not represent a legal and conforming use of the land.

We will not purchase a mortgage on a property if the improvements do not constitute a legally permissible use of the land. We will purchase a mortgage that is secured by a property that represents a legal, but non-conforming, use of the land as long as the appraiser's analysis reflects any adverse effect that the non-conforming use has on the property's value and marketability.

Section 405.02
Highest and Best Use

The highest and best use of a site is that reasonable and probable use that supports the highest present value on the effective date of the appraisal. For improvements to represent the highest and best use of a site, they must be legally permitted, be financially feasible, be physically possible, and provide more profit than any other use of the site would generate. All four of these criteria must be met if the improvements are to be considered as the highest and best use of a site.

A strict theoretical highest and best use analysis identifies the perfect improvements for a site—assuming that the site is vacant and available to be developed. The appraiser's highest and best use analysis of the subject property should consider the property as it is

Underwriting Guidelines
Property and Appraisal Analysis

Section 405.05 **Selling**

improved. This treatment recognizes that the existing improvements should continue in use until it is financially feasible to remove the dwelling and build a new one, or to renovate the existing dwelling. If the use of comparable sales demonstrates that the improvements are reasonably typical and compatible with market demand for the neighborhood, and the present improvements contribute to the value of the subject property so that its value is greater than the estimated vacant site value, the appraiser should consider the existing use as reasonable and report it as the highest and best use. On the other hand, if the current improvements clearly do not represent the highest and best use of the site as an improved site, the appraiser must so indicate on the appraisal report. In such cases, we will not purchase a mortgage that is secured by the subject property.

**Section 405.03
Utilities**

For a mortgage to be eligible for purchase, the security property's utilities must meet community standards and be accepted generally by area residents. If public sewer and/or water facilities—those that are supplied and regulated by the local government—are not available, then community or private well and septic facilities must be available and utilized by the subject property. Private well or septic facilities must be located on the subject site. If private community facilities are used, the owners of the subject property must have the right to access the system's facilities, which must be viable on an on-going basis.

If there is market resistance to an area because of environmental hazards or any other conditions that affect well, septic, or public water facilities, the appraiser must comment on the hazards' effect on the subject property's marketability and value.

**Section 405.04
Streets**

The property should front on a publicly dedicated and maintained street that meets community standards and is accepted generally by area residents. If the property is on a community-owned or privately owned and maintained street, there must be an adequate, legally enforceable agreement for maintenance of the street. A street that does not meet city or state standards frequently requires extensive maintenance, and property values may decline if it is not regularly maintained. If a property fronts on a street that is not typical of those found in the community, the appraiser must comment on the effect of that location on the subject property's marketability and value.

**Section 405.05
The Lot**

The topography, shape, size, and drainage of the lot are all equally important. Steep slopes that cause erosion, difficulty in maintaining a lawn, or difficult access to the property itself or to a garage are

Selling

Underwriting Guidelines
Property and Appraisal Analysis

Section 406.01

generally unfavorable conditions. Drainage must be away from the improvements to avoid the collection of water in or around them. The presence of sidewalks, curbs and gutters, street lights, and alleys depends on local custom—if they are typical in the community, they should be present on the subject site. The appraiser must comment on any adverse conditions and address their effect on the subject property's marketability and value.

Section 405.06
Flood Hazard Area

The appraiser must indicate whether or not the property is located in a special flood hazard area identified by the Federal Emergency Management Agency (FEMA).

Special flood hazard areas are identified on Flood Insurance Rate Maps (FIRM), which can be obtained by contacting FEMA at the following address or telephone numbers. FEMA requires that requests for more than five maps be in writing.

Federal Emergency Management Agency
Flood Map Distribution Center
6930 (A-F) San Tomas Road
Baltimore, MD 21227-6227

1-800-638-6620, for the Continental U.S.;
1-800-492-6605, for Maryland only;
1-800-638-6831, for Alaska, Hawaii, Puerto Rico, and Virgin Islands.

When the appraiser determines that a property is located in a special flood hazard area, he or she must indicate on the appraisal report form the map or community-panel number and the specific flood zone.

(also see Part III, Section 222)

If the appraiser indicates that the property improvements are located in a special flood hazard area—zones A, AO, AH, A1-30, A-99, V, or V1-30—flood insurance is required. If the land is in the hazard area, but the improvements are not, flood insurance is not required.

Section 406
Improvement Analysis

The appraiser must provide a clear, detailed, and accurate description of the improvements. The appraiser should be as specific as possible, and should provide supporting addenda if necessary. Lenders should pay particular attention to the following areas.

Section 406.01
Conformity To Neighborhood

The improvements should generally conform to the neighborhood in terms of age, type, design, and materials used for their construction. If there is market resistance to a property because its improvements are not compatible with the neighborhood or with the requirements of the competitive market—because of remaining economic life; adequacy of plumbing, heating, or electrical services; design; quality; size; condition; or any other reason directly related to market

Underwriting Guidelines
Property and Appraisal Analysis

Section 406.02

Selling

demand—the lender should underwrite the loan more carefully and, if appropriate, require more conservative mortgage terms. However, the lender should be aware that many older neighborhoods have favorable heterogeneity in architectural styles, land use, and age of housing. For example, older neighborhoods are especially likely to have been developed through custom building; this variety may be a positive marketing factor.

In the appraisal and underwriting process, special consideration must be given to properties that represent special or unique housing for the subject neighborhood. Non-traditional types of housing—such as earth houses, geodesic domes, log houses, etc.—or atypical types of housing for the neighborhood—such as a contemporary dwelling in a housing market that consists of traditional dwellings—must be reviewed with care. All properties must meet all local building codes and zoning ordinances. In addition, the appraiser must be able to establish that an active, viable market exists in order for the property to be eligible for maximum financing. If there is limited evidence of market acceptance, the lender must require more conservative mortgage terms. However, if the appraiser is not able to find any evidence of market acceptance and the characteristics of the property are so significant or so unique that he or she cannot establish a reliable estimate of market value, we will not accept the property as security for any mortgage.

We do not specify minimum size or living area requirements for properties. However, dwelling units of any type should contain sufficient living area to be acceptable to typical purchasers or tenants in the subject market area. There should be comparables of similar size to the subject property to support the general acceptability of a particular property type.

Section 406.02
Actual and Effective Ages

The relationship between the actual and effective ages of the property is a good indication of its condition. A property that has been well-maintained will generally have an effective age somewhat lower than its actual age. On the other hand, properties that have an effective age higher than their actual age probably have not been well-maintained or may have a particular physical problem. In such cases, the lender must pay particular attention to the condition of the subject property in its review of the appraisal.

(also see section 404.08 and 407.02)

We do not place a restriction on the age of eligible dwellings. Consequently, mortgages on older dwellings that meet our general requirements are acceptable. The improvements for all properties must be of the quality and condition that will meet local building codes and must be acceptable to typical purchasers in the subject market area.

	Underwriting Guidelines
	Property and Appraisal Analysis
Selling	Section 406.05

Section 406.03
Insulation and Energy Efficiency

(also see Sections 502 and 508)

The *Uniform Residential Appraisal Report* (Form 1004) provides an area for the appraiser to state the "R" value for insulation if he or she is aware of it and to comment on the adequacy of the insulation. Then, in the "sales comparison analysis" grid, the appraiser also should list the energy-efficient items to reflect the overall contribution of these items to the market value of the subject property.

An energy-efficient property is one that uses cost-effective design, materials, equipment, and site orientation to conserve nonrenewable fuels. Special energy saving items should be recognized in the appraisal process. The nature of these items and their contribution to value will vary throughout the country because of climatic conditions and differences in utility costs.

Section 406.04
Layout and Floor Plans

Dwellings with unusual layouts, peculiar floor plans, or inadequate equipment or amenities generally have limited market appeal and should not be considered for maximum financing. A review of the room list and floor plan for the dwelling unit may indicate an unusual layout—such as bedrooms on a level with no bath, or a kitchen on a different level from the dining room. If the appraiser indicates that such inadequacies result in market resistance to the property, he or she should make appropriate adjustments to reflect this in the overall analysis. On the other hand, if market acceptance can be demonstrated through the use of comparable sales with the same inadequacies, no adjustments are required.

Section 406.05
Room List and Gross Living Area

Both the *Uniform Residential Appraisal Report* (Form 1004) and the *Appraisal Report—Individual Condominium or PUD Unit* (Form 1073) contain a "room list" section to describe the subject property. In addition, the Form 1004 provides a column for the gross living area per level, as well as space for a summary of the total above-grade room count and the above-grade gross living area.

The appraiser must be consistent when he or she calculates and reports the finished above-grade room count and the square feet of gross living area that is above-grade. For units in condominum or cooperative projects, the appraiser should use interior perimeter unit dimensions to calculate the gross living area. In all other instances, the appraiser should use the exterior building dimensions per floor to calculate a property's above-grade gross living area. Only finished above-grade areas should be used—garages and basements (including those that are partially above-grade) should not be included. We consider a level to be below-grade if any portion of it is below-grade—regardless of the quality of its "finish" or the window area of any room. Therefore, a walk-out basement with finished rooms would not be included in the above-grade room count.

Underwriting Guidelines
Property and Appraisal Analysis

Section 407.01

Selling

Rooms that are not included in the above-grade room count may add substantially to the value of a property—particularly when the quality of the "finish" is high. For that reason, the appraiser should report the basement or other partially below-grade areas separately and make appropriate adjustments for them on the "basement and finished areas below-grade" line in the "sales comparison analysis" adjustment grid. To assure consistency in the sales comparison analysis, the appraiser should compare above-grade areas to above-grade areas and below-grade areas to below-grade areas. However, if the appraiser needs to deviate from this approach because of the style of the subject property or of any of the comparables, he or she must explain the reason for the deviation and clearly describe the comparisons that are being made.

Section 406.06 Infestation, Dampness, or Settlement

If the appraiser indicates that there is evidence of dampness, wood-boring insects, or settlement, he or she must comment on its effect on the subject property's marketability and value. The lender must provide either satisfactory evidence that the condition was corrected or submit a professionally prepared report, which indicates that—based on an inspection of the property—the condition does not pose any threat of structural damage to the improvements.

Section 407 Property Condition and Appraiser Comments

Based on the factual data of the improvement analysis, the appraiser must express an opinion about the condition of the improvements. This opinion should be descriptive and should support the summary shown in the "improvement analysis" rating.

Section 407.01 Improvement Analysis Rating

Our appraisal report forms provide a summary of the principal factors about the improvements that have a bearing on the value and marketability of the subject property. These factors are rated to indicate how the subject property compares to competing properties in the general market area. The same ratings that were used in Section 404.09 to summarize the neighborhood analysis—good, average, fair, and poor—must be used to summarize the improvement analysis.

A less-than-"average" rating indicates that the rated item is inferior to that in competing properties in the subject market area and, as such, will probably result in the subject property's meeting with buyer resistance. If any items are rated less-than-"average", the appraiser must comment on the reasons for the rating and on how they affect the marketability and value of the subject property. The lender's underwriter must consider the relative significance of the items rated as less-than-"average". A property that has limited marketability is not eligible for maximum financing—to be eligible, the improvements should generally be rated as, at least, "average".

Selling

Underwriting Guidelines
Property and Appraisal Analysis

Section 407.02

The appraiser must report the condition of the improvements in factual, specific terms. The use of ratings does not preclude an appraiser from reporting the detrimental condition of improvements even if that condition is also typical for competing properties. Any condition that may affect the value or marketability of the subject property must be reported to assure that the appraiser adequately describes the property. For instance, the appraiser should note if a property is characterized by deferred maintenance or a lack of updating even if the same condition applies to competing properties in the neighborhood.

**Section 407.02
Remaining Economic Life**

The remaining economic life of a property is the estimated period over which the improvements will continue to contribute to the value of the property, or the estimated period in which the improvements increase the value of the property above that for the vacant site. Four basic forces influence real property values—social standards, economic factors, government controls, and environmental conditions. Because these forces may result in a change in the improvements' contribution to value, estimating the remaining economic life of a property can be difficult. Therefore, the appraiser should emphasize the overall quality and design of the improvements and the attitudes of typical purchasers in the subject market area. The appraiser may state the remaining economic life as a single figure or as a range (when that is more appropriate).

Generally, the mortgage term should not exceed the appraiser's estimate of the remaining economic life for the subject property. However, a remaining economic life that is less than the term of the mortgage may be acceptable if the improvements represent a fairly typical residential property for the neighborhood, rather than a speculative land or land-development-type property. In such cases, the reason for the shorter remaining economic life must be the result of economic factors (which would increase the value of the site), rather than the result of the physical deterioration or condition of the improvements. We will not purchase any mortgage that is secured by a property that does not have a minimum remaining economic life that is at least equal to one-half of the term of the mortgage.

Because the *Uniform Residential Appraisal Report* (Form 1004) was designed to meet the needs of several different user groups, it also includes a space to insert the property's estimated remaining physical life. The remaining physical life of a property is the estimated period over which the improvements will physically last if they receive normal maintenance. For mortgages that will be sold to Fannie Mae, the appraiser does not need to report the remaining physical life—"N/A" may be inserted in that space. If the appraiser does report the remaining physical life, the lender does not need to consider it, because any related property deficiencies will be dis-

Underwriting Guidelines
Property and Appraisal Analysis

Section 408.01

Selling

cussed in the sections of the appraisal report that address economic life, the improvement analysis, and comments on the property's condition.

Section 407.03
Appraiser's Comments

The appraiser must address any needed repairs or any physical, functional, or external inadequacies in the "Comments" section. In addition, the appraiser should also include comments related to general market conditions in the subject market area in the space provided for that purpose on the *Uniform Residential Appraisal Report* (Form 1004).

Section 408
Valuation Analysis

The valuation section of our appraisal report form enables appraisers to develop and report in concise format an adequately supported estimate of market value—based on the cost, sales comparison, and income approaches to value. However, if the appraiser believes that additional information needs to be provided because of the uniqueness of the property or some other condition, he or she should provide the additional supporting data in an addendum to the appraisal report form.

Section 408.01
Cost Approach

The cost approach to value assumes that a potential purchaser will consider building a substitute residence that has the same use as the property that is being appraised. This approach, then, measures value as a cost of production. The reliability of the cost approach depends on valid reproduction cost estimates, proper depreciation estimates, and accurate site values.

Since units in condominium and cooperative projects are integral parts of the total project, the cost approach is generally impractical for determining the value of any given unit; therefore, the appraiser does not have to consider the cost approach when appraising these units. Usually, the cost approach is a good indicator of value for newer or renovated properties that are one- to four-family residences or units in PUD or *de minimis* PUD projects. However, as the effective age of a property increases, the reliability of the cost approach may decrease because the depreciation estimates may be subjective. We will not accept appraisals that rely solely on the cost approach as an indicator of market value.

A. Determining the indicated value. There are three principal types of depreciation—physical, functional, and external—that the appraiser must consider:

Physical depreciation—traditionally referred to as physical deterioration—is a loss in value that is caused by deterioration in the physical condition of the improvements. Appraisers classify physical deterioration as "curable" or "incurable". Curable physical

Selling

Underwriting Guidelines
Property and Appraisal Analysis

Section 408.01

deterioration refers to items of deferred maintenance—for example, painting or items currently in need of repair (such as broken stair rails). Incurable physical deterioration refers to other items that currently are not practical or feasible to correct—for example, furnaces or roof shingles that have not reached the end of their economic life.

Functional depreciation—traditionally referred to as functional obsolescence—is a loss in value that is caused by defects in the design of the structure—for example, inadequacies in such items as architecture, floor plan, or sizes and types of rooms. It also can be caused by changes in market preferences that result in some aspect of the improvements being considered obsolete by current standards—for example, the location of a bedroom on a level with no bathroom, or access to a bedroom only through another bedroom.

External depreciation—traditionally referred to as economic obsolescence—is a loss in value that is caused by negative influences that are outside of the site, such as economic factors or environmental changes—for example, shopping centers, expressways, or factories that are adjacent to the subject property.

The appraiser arrives at the indicated value of a property by estimating the reproduction cost of new improvements, subtracting the amount of depreciation from all causes, and adding an estimate of the value for the site if it were vacant and available to be developed to its highest and best use. The reproduction cost estimate should reflect the cost of construction based on the current prices of producing a replica of the property being appraised—including all of its positive and negative characteristics. Although the construction materials used for the estimate should be as similar as possible to those used for the subject property, they do not have to be exactly the same.

If the appraiser's estimate of the value for the site is one that is not typical for a comparable residential property in the subject neighborhood, he or she must comment on how the variance affects the marketability of the subject property.

B. Appraiser's comments and adjustments. In reviewing the appraisal report, the lender should make sure that the appraiser's analysis in the cost approach is consistent with comments and adjustments mentioned elsewhere in the report. For example, if the neighborhood or site description reveals that the property backs up to a shopping center, the lender should expect to see an adjustment for external depreciation in the cost approach. Similarly, if the improvement analysis indicates that it is necessary to go through one bedroom to get to another bedroom, the lender should expect to see an adjustment for functional depreciation.

Underwriting Guidelines
Property and Appraisal Analysis

Section 408.02

Selling

Section 408.02
Sales Comparison
Approach

(Also see Section 402.02)

The sales comparison approach to value—traditionally referred to as the market data approach—is an analysis of comparable sales, contract offerings, and current listings of properties that are the most comparable to the subject property. However, we require the appraiser to report only the comparable sales in the appraisal report. The comparable sales must be verified, analyzed, and adjusted for differences between the comparable properties and the subject property. Because the appraiser's estimate of market value is no better than the reliability of the comparable data that is used, the appraiser must exercise due diligence to ensure the reliability of the comparable sales data that he or she uses. When comparable sales data is provided by a party that has a financial interest in either the sale or financing of the subject property, the appraiser must reverify the data with a party who does not have a financial interest in the subject transaction.

A. Selecting the comparables. The appraiser must report a minimum of three comparable sales as part of the sales comparison approach. The appraiser may submit more than three comparable sales to support his or her estimate of market value, as long as at least three are actual settled or closed sales. Generally, the appraiser should use comparable sales that have been settled or closed within the last 12 months. However, the appraiser may use older comparable sales as additional supporting data if he or she believes that it is appropriate. The appraiser must comment on the reasons for using any comparable sales that are more than six months old. In addition, the appraiser may use the subject property as a fourth comparable sale or as supporting data if the property previously was sold (and closed or settled). If the appraiser believes that it is appropriate, he or she also may use contract offerings and current listings as supporting data.

For properties that are in established subdivisions or projects that have resale activity, the appraiser should use comparable sales from within the subject property's subdivision or project if there are any available. Resale activity from within the subdivision or project should be the best indicator of value for properties in that subdivision or project. If the appraiser uses sales of comparable properties that are located outside of the subject neighborhood, he or she must include an explanation with the analysis.

For properties in new subdivisions or for units in new (or recently converted) condominium, PUD, or *de minimis* PUD projects, the appraiser must compare the subject property to other properties in its general market area as well as to properties within the subject subdivision or project. This comparison should help demonstrate market acceptance of new developments and the properties within them. Generally, the appraiser should select one comparable sale from the subject subdivision or project, one comparable sale from outside the

Underwriting Guidelines
Property and Appraisal Analysis

Selling

Section 408.02

subject subdivision or project, and one comparable sale, which can be from inside or outside of the subject subdivision or project as long as the appraiser considers it to be a good indicator of value for the subject property. In selecting the comparables, the appraiser should keep in mind that resales from within the subject subdivision or project are preferable to sales from outside the subdivision or project as long as the developer or builder of the subject property is not involved in the transactions.

B. Adjustments to comparable sales. Each comparable sale that is used in the sales comparison approach must be analyzed for differences and similarities between it and the property that is being appraised. The appraiser must make appropriate adjustments for location, terms and conditions of sale, date of sale, and the physical characteristics of the properties. "Time" adjustments must be representative of the market and should be supported by the comparable sales whenever possible. The adjustments must reflect the time that elapsed between the contract date (or the date of the "meeting of the minds") for the comparable sale and the effective date of the appraisal for the subject property.

Comparable sales must be adjusted *to* the subject property—except for sales and financing concessions, which are adjusted to the market at the time of sale. The subject property is the standard against which the comparable sales are evaluated and adjusted. Thus, if an item in the comparable property is superior to that in the subject property, a minus (–) adjustment is required to make that item equal to that in the subject property. Conversely, if an item in the comparable property is inferior to that in the subject property, a plus (+) adjustment is required to make that item equal to that in the subject property.

The proper selection of comparable properties minimizes both the need for, and the size of, any dollar adjustments. Occasionally, there may be no similar or truly comparable sales for a particular property—because of the uniqueness of the property or other conditions. In such cases, the appraiser must use his or her knowledge and judgment to select comparable sales that represent the best indicators of value for the subject property and to make adjustments to reflect the actions of typical purchasers in that market. Dollar adjustments should reflect the market's reaction to the difference in the properties, not necessarily the cost of the difference. Swimming pools, electronic air filters, intercom systems, elaborately finished basements, carpets, and other special features generally do not affect value to the extent of their cost.

We have established guidelines for the net and gross percentage adjustments that underwriters may rely on as a general indicator of whether a property should be used as a comparable sale. Generally,

Underwriting Guidelines
Property and Appraisal Analysis

Section 408.02

Selling

the dollar amount of the net adjustments for each comparable sale should not exceed 15% of the comparable's sales price. When the adjustments exceed 15%, the appraiser must comment on the reasons for not using a more similar comparable. Further, the dollar amount of the gross adjustments for each comparable sale should not exceed 25% of the comparable's sales price. The amount of the gross adjustment is determined by adding all individual adjustments without regard to the plus or minus signs. When the adjustments exceed 25%, the appraiser must comment on the reasons for not using a more similar comparable. Individual adjustments that are excessively high should be explained by the appraiser and reviewed carefully by the lender's underwriter. In some circumstances, the use of comparables with higher-than-normal adjustments may be warranted, but the appraiser must satisfactorily justify his or her use of them.

The appraiser must research the market and select the most comparable sales that are available for the subject property, and then adjust them to reflect the market's reaction to the differences (except for sales and financing concessions) between the comparable sales and the subject property, without regard for the percentage or amount of the dollar adjustments. If the appraiser's adjustments do not fall within our net and gross percentage adjustment guidelines, but the appraiser believes that the comparable sales used in the analysis are the best available, as well as the best indicators of value for the subject property, the appraiser simply has to provide an appropriate explanation. If the extent of the appraiser's adjustments to the comparable sales is great enough to indicate that the property may not conform to the general market area, the lender's underwriter must give special consideration to the case. An atypical property might require more conservative mortgage terms because it might not be appealing to a typical purchaser in the market area.

C. **Sales comparison analysis adjustment grid.** The lender's underwriter should review thoroughly the "sales comparison analysis" adjustment grid. The sales comparison analysis provides many places in which an error can be made in the use of dollar adjustments. A spotcheck must always be made of the adjustment calculations and the use of plus (+) and minus (-) signs. Errors in arithmetic may have a significant effect on the value conclusion and are, therefore, reason for the lender to contact the appraiser.

The underwriter should pay particular attention to the following items. Because a substantial variance raises questions about the validity of using a specific comparable sale, the appraiser should address the reason for a variance.

Selling

Underwriting Guidelines
Property and Appraisal Analysis

Section 408.02

1. Proximity to subject property, and location. The description of the comparable's proximity to the subject property must be specific (e.g., two blocks south). Whenever possible, the appraiser should use comparable sales in the same neighborhood as the subject property because the sales prices of comparable properties in the neighborhood should reflect the same positive and negative locational characteristics.

2. Sales price. The sales price of each comparable sale should be within the general range of the estimate of market value for the subject property. A $100,000 comparable sale for a $75,000 subject property would raises questions about the validity of the comparable.

3. Sales or financing concessions. The dollar amount of sales or financing concessions paid by the seller must be reported for the comparables if the information is reasonably available. Generally, sales or financing data for comparable sales—such as the mortgage amount, loan type, interest rate, term, and any fees or concessions the seller paid—is available. The appraiser should obtain this information from an individual who was a party to the comparable transaction (the broker, buyer, or seller) or from a data source that the appraiser considers to be reliable. We recognize that there may be some situations in which sales or financing information is not available because of legal restrictions or other disclosure-related problems. In such cases, the appraiser must explain why the information is not available—however, we will not accept an explanation that indicates that the appraiser did not make an effort to verify the information. In all other cases, the appraiser must provide the sales and financing concession information that was available (and verified) for the comparables. If the appraisal report form does not provide enough space to discuss this information, the appraiser should make adjustments for the concessions on the form and explain them in an addendum to the appraisal report.

Examples of sales or financing concessions include interest rate buydowns or other below-market rate financing; loan discount points; loan origination fees; closing costs customarily paid by the buyer; payment of condominium or PUD association fees; refunds of (or credit for) the borrower's expenses; absorption of monthly payments; assignment of rent payments; and the inclusion of non-realty items in the transaction. The amount of the negative adjustment to be made to each comparable with sales or financing concessions is equal to any increase in the purchase price of the comparable that the appraiser determines to be attributable to the concessions.

The need to make negative adjustments and the amount of the adjustments to the comparables for sales and financing concessions

Underwriting Guidelines
Property and Appraisal Analysis

Section 408.02

Selling

are not based on how typical the concessions might be for a segment of the market area—large sales concessions can be relatively typical in a particular segment of the market and still result in sale prices that reflect more than the value of the real estate. Adjustments based on mechanical, dollar-for-dollar, deductions that are equal to the cost of the concessions to the seller (as a strict cash equivalency approach would dictate) are not appropriate. We recognize that the effect of the sales concessions on sales prices can vary with the amount of the concessions and differences in various markets. The adjustments must reflect the difference between what the comparables actually sold for with the sales concessions and what they would have sold for without the concessions so that the dollar amount of the adjustments will approximate the market's reaction to the concessions.

Positive adjustments for sales or financing concessions are not acceptable. For example, if local tradition or law results in virtually all of the property sellers in the market area paying a 1% loan origination fee for the purchaser, and a property seller in that market did not pay any loan fees or concessions for the purchaser, the sale would be considered as a cash equivalent sale in that market. The appraiser should recognize comparable sales that sold for all cash or with cash equivalent financing and use them as comparables if they are the best indicators of value for the subject property. Such sales can also be useful to the appraiser in determining those costs that are normally paid by sellers as the result of tradition or law in the market area.

4. Date of sale/time adjustment. We will accept more than three comparable sales as part of the appraisal report, but at least three of them must be actual settled or closed sales. The appraiser should provide the date of the sales contract and the settlement or closing date for each comparable sale. Unless the appraiser believes that the exact date is necessary to understand the adjustments, only the month and year of the sale need to be reported. If the appraiser does not report both the contract date and the settlement or closing date, he or she must identify the reported sale date as either the "contract date" or the "settlement or closing date". If the appraiser reports the contract date only, he or she must state whether the contract resulted in a settlement or a closing.

5. Above-grade room count and gross living area. Only finished above-grade areas should be included in the calculation of the gross living area. The appraiser should report the basement and other partially below-grade areas separately and adjust for them accordingly. The room count and gross living area should be similar for the subject property and all comparables. For example, a four bedroom comparable sale generally is not acceptable to support the

Selling

Underwriting Guidelines
Property and Appraisal Analysis

Section 408.03

value of a two bedroom subject property. The appraiser must address large differences between the subject property and the comparable sales, since they raise doubts about the validity of the comparables as good indicators of value.

6. Over-improvements. In some instances, the improvements can represent an over-improvement for the neighborhood, but still be within the neighborhood price range—such as a property with an in-ground swimming pool, a large addition, or an oversized garage in a market that does not demand these kinds of improvements. The appraiser must comment on such over-improvements and indicate their contributory value in the "sales comparison analysis" adjustment grid.

Because an over-improved property may not be acceptable to the typical purchaser, the lender's underwriter must review appraisals on this type of property carefully to ensure that the appraiser has reflected only the contributory value of the over-improvement in his or her analysis.

D. Appraiser's comments and indicated value. The appraiser's comments should reflect his or her reconciliation of the adjusted (or indicated) values for the comparable sales and identify the comparable(s) that were given the most weight in arriving at the indicated value for the subject property.

Section 408.03 Income Approach

The income approach to value is based on the assumption that market value is related to the market rent or income that a property can be expected to earn. Its use generally is appropriate in neighborhoods of single-family properties when there is a substantial rental market, and it is an important approach in the valuation of a two- to four-family property. However, it generally is not appropriate in areas that consist mostly of owner-occupied properties since adequate rental data generally does not exist for those areas. We will not accept an appraisal if the appraiser relies solely on the income approach as an indicator of market value.

To arrive at the indicated value by the income approach, the appraiser multiplies the estimated market rent for the subject property by a gross rent multiplier.

- *Estimated market rent* is based on an analysis of comparable rentals in the neighborhood. After appropriate adjustments are made to the comparables, their adjusted (or indicated) values are reconciled to develop an estimated monthly market rent for the subject property.

- The *gross rent multiplier* is determined by dividing the sales prices of comparable properties that were rented at the time of

Underwriting Guidelines
Property and Appraisal Analysis

Section 410

Selling

sale by their monthly market rent, which is then reconciled to create a single gross rent multiplier (or a range of multipliers) for the subject property.

When the property being appraised is a single-family property that will be used as an investment property, the appraiser must prepare a *Single-Family Comparable Rent Schedule* (Form 1007) in addition to the appropriate appraisal report form. This form is not required for a two- to four-family property since the *Appraisal Report—Small Residential Income Property* (Form 1025) provides substantially the same information. When the appraiser is relying on the income approach, he or she should attach the supporting comparable rental and sales data, and the calculations used to determine the gross rent multiplier, as an addendum to the appraisal report form.

**Section 409
Final Reconciliation**

The reconciliation process that leads to the estimate of market value is an on-going process throughout the appraiser's analysis. In the final reconciliation, the appraiser must reconcile the reasonableness and reliability of each approach to value and the reasonableness and validity of the indicated values and the available data, and then must select and report the approach or approaches that were given the most weight. The final reconciliation must never be an averaging technique.

If the appraiser has provided a comprehensive and logical analysis of the neighborhood and the property, the lender's underwriter should be able to reach a sound conclusion on the adequacy of the property as security for the mortgage.

**Section 410
Appraiser's Certification**

We will not purchase a mortgage unless the appraisal is based on our *Certification and Statement of Limiting Conditions* (Form 1004B), as it was revised in July, 1986. To acknowledge that the current version of the Form 1004B was used and to assure the lender that the appraiser is certifying to our current definition of value, the appraiser must

- check the box in the "Reconciliation" section of the *Uniform Residential Appraisal Report* (Form 1004) that references "Freddie Mac Form 439 (Rev. 7/86), Fannie Mae Form 1004B (Rev. 7/86). . . ."; or

- check the box at the bottom of the *Appraisal Report—Small Residential Income Property* (Form 1025), the *Appraisal Report—Individual Condominium or PUD Unit* (Form 1073), or the *Loan Valuation Summary for Second Mortgages* (Form 219), that references the Freddie Mac Form 439/Fannie Mae Form 1004B, and correct any references to the outdated version of Form 1004B by striking the earlier revision date and replacing it with a "07/86" date.

Selling

Underwriting Guidelines
Property and Appraisal Analysis

Section 410.01

Section 410.01
Definition of Market Value

Fannie Mae's definition of market value is intended to assure that appraisals reflect an estimate of market value after adjustments for any special or creative financing or sales concessions—such as seller contributions, interest rate buydowns, etc.—have been made.

The appraiser must certify that he or she uses the following definition of market value (which is stated in the 07/86 version of Form 1004B):

Market value is the most probable price which a property should bring in a competitive and open market under all conditions requisite to a fair sale, the buyer and seller, each acting prudently, knowledgeably and assuming the price is not affected by undue stimulus. Implicit in this definition is the consummation of a sale as of a specified date and the passing of title from seller to buyer under conditions whereby: (1) buyer and seller are typically motivated; (2) both parties are well informed or well advised, and each acting in what he considers his own best interest; (3) a reasonable time is allowed for exposure in the open market; (4) payment is made in terms of cash in U.S. dollars or in terms of financial arrangements comparable thereto; and (5) the price represents the normal consideration for the property sold unaffected by special or creative financing or sales concessions* granted by anyone associated with the sale.

(also see section 408.04)

*Adjustments to the comparables must be made for special or creative financing or sales concessions. No adjustments are necessary for those costs which are normally paid by sellers as a result of tradition or law in a market area; these costs are readily identifiable since the seller pays these costs in virtually all sales transactions. Special or creative financing adjustments can be made to the comparable property by comparisons to financing terms offered by a third party institutional lender that is not already involved in the property or transaction. Any adjustment should not be calculated on a mechanical dollar for dollar cost of the financing or concession but the dollar amount of any adjustment should approximate the market's reaction to the financing or concessions based on the appraiser's judgment.

The asterisked section of the definition provides consistent interpretation for appraisers. Specifically, we want to emphasize that the phrases "...those costs which are normally paid by sellers as a result of tradition or law in a market area; these costs are readily identifiable since the seller pays these costs in virtually all sales transactions..." refer to all of the sellers in a specific market area.

Underwriting Guidelines
Property and Appraisal Analysis

Section 410.02

Selling

No distinction is made between a specific group of sellers, builders, developers, or individuals in the resale market—they are all considered to be individual sellers in the market. To illustrate: When a property seller is paying part of the purchaser's settlement or closing costs—or is paying for an interest-rate buydown or other below-market financing—but virtually all of the other sellers in the market are *not* doing the same as a result of law or tradition, the appraiser would need to make an adjustment even if there are other groups of sellers—such as builders—who are also offering concessionary financing.

The appraiser can adjust a comparable property that has special or creative financing or sales concessions by comparing it to other properties that had financing terms offered by a third party institutional lender—as long as that lender is not already involved in the subject property or transaction. The appraiser should use his or her judgment in establishing the dollar amount for any adjustment to assure that it approximates the market's reaction to the financing or concession at the time of the sale.

Section 410.02 Certifications

The appraiser must agree to a number of certifications, which are contained in detail in the *Certification and Statement of Limiting Conditions* (Form 1004B). Those certifications are summarized below.

1. The appraiser must certify that he or she has no present, or contemplated future, interest in the subject property, and his or her employment or payment for making the appraisal is not contingent on the appraised value of the property.

2. The appraiser must certify that he or she has no personal interest or bias with respect to the subject matter of the appraisal report or to the participants in the sale, and that he or she will not base—either partially or completely—the "estimate of market value" in the appraisal report on the race, color, or national origin of either the prospective owners or occupants of the subject property or of the present owners or occupants of the properties in the vicinity of the subject property.

3. The appraiser must certify that he or she has personally inspected the inside and outside of the subject property and the outside of all comparable sales listed in the appraisal report; believes, to the best of his or her knowledge, that the information in the appraisal report is true and correct; and has not knowingly withheld any significant information.

4. The appraiser must certify that he or she has included all contingent and limiting conditions—which were imposed by the

Selling

Underwriting Guidelines
Property and Appraisal Analysis

Section 410.03

terms of the assignment or developed as the result of his or her opinions, analyses, and conclusions—in the appraisal report.

5. The appraiser must certify that he or she has performed the appraisal in conformity with, and subject to, the requirements of the Code of Professional Ethics and Standards of Professional Conduct of the appraisal organizations with which the appraiser is affiliated.

6. The appraiser must certify that he or she has personally prepared all of the conclusions and opinions concerning the real estate that were set out in the appraisal report (unless he or she signed the report only as a "Review Appraiser"), agrees that no one else may change any item in the appraisal report, and indicates that he or she will not be responsible for any unauthorized changes.

Section 410.03 Contingent and Limiting Conditions

The appraiser's certifications are subject to a number of conditions. The specific contingent and limiting conditions appear in the *Certification and Statement of Limiting Conditions* (Form 1004B); however, they are summarized below.

1. The appraiser will not be responsible for matters of a legal nature that affect the property being appraised, or the title to it. Since the property is appraised on the basis of it being under responsible ownership, the appraiser assumes that the title is good and marketable and will not render any opinions about the title.

2. The appraiser has made no survey of the property; therefore, any sketch in the report shows approximate dimensions and is included only to assist the reader of the report in visualizing the property.

3. The appraiser will not give testimony or appear in court because he or she made an appraisal of the property in question, unless specific arrangements to do so have been made beforehand.

4. The appraiser has distributed the value of the property between the land and the improvements on the basis of the existing use of the property. These separate valuations must not be used in conjunction with any other appraisal and are invalid if they are so used.

5. The appraiser has assumed that there are no hidden or unapparent conditions of the property, the subsoil, or the structures that would make the property more or less valuable. The appraiser will not be responsible for any such conditions that do exist or for any engineering that might be required to discover whether such factors exist.

Underwriting Guidelines
Property and Appraisal Analysis

Section 410.03

Selling

6. The appraiser obtained the information, estimates, and opinions that were expressed in the appraisal report from sources that he or she considers to be reliable and believes them to be true and correct. The appraiser does not assume responsibility for the accuracy of such items that were furnished by other parties.

7. The appraiser will not disclose the contents of the appraisal report except as provided for in the Bylaws and Regulations of the professional appraisal organizations with which he or she is affiliated.

8. The appraiser must provide his or her prior written consent before all (or any part) of the content of the appraisal report—including conclusions about the property's value; the appraiser's identity and professional designations; and references to any professional appraisal organizations or the firm with which the appraiser is associated—can be used for any purposes by anyone except the client specified in the report; the borrower if he or she paid the appraisal fee; the mortgagee or its successors and assigns; mortgage insurers; consultants; professional appraisal organizations; any state- or federally approved financial institution; or any department, agency, or instrumentality of the United States or any state or the District of Columbia. The appraiser's written consent and approval must also be obtained before the appraisal (or any part of it) can be conveyed by anyone to the public through advertising, public relations, news, sales, or other media.

9. The appraiser has based his or her appraisal report and valuation conclusion for an appraisal that is subject to satisfactory completion, repairs, or alterations on the assumption that completion of the improvements will be performed in a workmanlike manner.

	Underwriting Guidelines
Selling	Special Considerations
	Section 501.02

Chapter 5. Special Considerations

This Chapter addresses special underwriting and appraisal requirements that apply only to certain types of mortgages or properties. Unless we indicate otherwise, our normal requirements also apply to these mortgages or properties.

Section 501
Special Underwriting Considerations

Some types of mortgages or properties may require a slightly modified approach to underwriting because they require different documentation or have features that are not usually considered during the normal course of underwriting.

Section 501.01
VA Mortgages on Two-to Four-Family Properties

We will accept VA's credit documentation—*Application for Home Loan Guaranty* (VA Form 26-1802a), *Verification of Deposit* (VA Form 26-8497a), and *Verification of Employment* (VA Form 26-8497)—in lieu of the standard documentation that we normally require. The application form must be completed in all cases, even though VA does not require its use for mortgages closed under the automatic processing program.

If the applicant has rental income from other real estate, we require additional documentation to justify recognition of the net income because VA's application does not provide sufficient information on this. The documentation should provide information on the gross income, mortgage payments, operating expenses, and the net income.

In addition to the *Certificate of Reasonable Value* (VA Form 26-1843) or the *Master Certificate of Reasonable Value* (VA Form 26-1843a), we require an independent appraisal on our form—the *Appraisal Report-Small Residential Income Property* (Form 1025).

Although we generally will consider purchasing mortgages on older dwellings, we will not purchase a mortgage that has a term greater than VA's estimate of the property's remaining economic life.

Section 501.02
Converted Adjustable Rate Mortgages

Lenders must give special underwriting consideration to mortgages that were originated as adjustable rate mortgages but which have been converted subsequently to fixed-rate mortgages. The lender can use the original in-file documentation to evaluate the borrower's financial ability as long as the borrower is able to qualify for the mortgage based on either

- the mortgage interest rate in effect following the conversion and our current underwriting guidelines for fixed-rate mortgages, or
- the mortgage interest rate in effect for the adjustable rate mortgage when it was originated and the ARM underwriting guidelines that we used at that time.

Underwriting Guidelines

Special Considerations

Section 501.03

Selling

If the borrower is unable to qualify for the mortgage under either of these options, the lender must obtain a new application and up-to-date credit reports and employment and income verifications. Generally, the lender may accept as verification of income and employment current pay stubs or telephone contact with the borrower's employer. If the borrower is not a salaried employee or is self-employed, the lender should obtain copies of signed Federal tax returns for the two years preceding the date the mortgage was converted to a fixed-rate mortgage. All written documentation regarding these verifications should be maintained in the individual mortgage file.

After it receives the required documentation, the lender should evaluate the borrower's financial ability based on the mortgage interest rate in effect for the converted mortgage and on our current underwriting guidelines for fixed-rate mortgages.

Section 501.03
Cooperative Unit
Mortgages

(also see
Section 502.01)

In the cooperative form of ownership, a corporation holds title to a residential project and sells shares of stock that give the purchasers the right to occupy the individual units in the project. Because a stockholder in a cooperative project pays his or her proportionate share of the debt and real estate taxes that are incurred by the corporation, the requirements for the project's blanket mortgage and the cooperative corporation must be considered in the underwriting process.

The evaluation of the borrower's creditworthiness must include a determination of the borrower's ability to handle monthly payment increases. The lender must consider any blanket mortgage or cooperative corporation expenses, in addition to any payment adjustments related to the unit mortgage. The blanket mortgage's type and terms must be documented. Particular attention must be paid to blanket mortgages that have an adjustable rate feature or a balloon payment because those features could result in a possible increase in the monthly debt service. The lender should also consider the adequacy of the cooperative corporation's replacement and operating reserves. If the reserves are inadequate, the borrower's payments to the cooperative corporation may increase because of special assessments or additional blanket financing.

The lender must be aware of whether the cooperative qualifies as a "cooperative housing corporation" under Section 216 of the Internal Revenue Service Code. If cooperative projects comply with Section 216, unit owners can take advantage of an income tax deduction for their share of the corporation's real estate taxes and interest payments on the blanket mortgage. The cooperative corporation must provide the lender with a statement about the corporation's compliance with Section 216. If the cooperative project does not meet

Underwriting Guidelines

Special Considerations

Section 501.04

Selling

Section 216 requirements, the lender cannot consider favorable tax consequences in the underwriting process.

The carrying charges—the unit owner's cooperative association fee—that the tenant-stockholder must contribute must be considered as a housing expense. The monthly fee, less the unit's pro rata share of the master utility charges for utilities that service individual units, must be included in the total monthly housing expense-to-income ratio.

**Section 501.04
Second Mortgages**

The lender must use our standard underwriting documentation, unless we have given prior approval for the use of equivalent forms. The following variations to our standard documentation also are acceptable:

- Either the *Second Mortgage or Home Improvement Loan Application* (Form 1012) or the *Residential Loan Application* (Form 1003) is acceptable;

- An "in-file" credit report is acceptable for all mortgages if the public records are reviewed. The review may be made by the credit reporting agency, the title company, or the lender. If a check of the public records is not made, an "in-file" credit report is acceptable only for mortgages that have unpaid balances of $30,000 or less. When discrepancies that cannot be satisfactorily verified or explained arise, we require a standard factual data credit report;

- *Loan Valuation Summary for Second Mortgages* (Form 219) may be used for single-family mortgages that have an unpaid balance of $15,000 or less. Our regular appraisal report forms must be used for single-family mortgages that have balances over $15,000, for two- to four-family properties, and for units in condominium or PUD projects.

Because a second lien generally involves more risk than a first lien, we apply stricter underwriting standards for second mortgages. We place greater reliance on the borrower's motive for borrowing and his or her present and future ability to repay both the first and second mortgages. Even though we do not restrict the use of the loan proceeds, the lender should consider the purpose of the loan. A second mortgage that increases or retains the borrower's investment in the property creates a strong motivation for repayment of the debt. A second mortgage that is used to bail a borrower out from under increasing liabilities by refinancing and consolidating debts is a marginal risk.

Underwriting Guidelines

Special Considerations

Section 501.05

Selling

The lender must pay close attention to the borrower's total obligations-to-income ratio and generally should not approve a mortgage if the ratio exceeds 36%. The lender also should consider the amount of income that the borrower will have available for living expenses after all obligations have been met. A borrower whose ability to meet living expenses appears questionable should be carefully evaluated.

The lender also must review the terms of the first mortgage and the borrower's payment history. The first mortgage instrument should be examined to determine if placing a second mortgage without the first lienholder's consent is a default. When such terms exist, the lender must obtain the lienholder's consent before it approves the second mortgage. When the first mortgage involves financing in which the monthly payments can increase—such as adjustable rate mortgages, graduated payment mortgages or mortgages subject to interest rate buydown plans—the lender should consider

- the borrower's ability to repay both mortgages, particularly at the point when the terms of the first mortgage call for a large payment increase;
- the unpredictability of interest rate changes and their effect on future housing expenses; and
- the borrower's job stability and cash reserves.

Section 501.05
Energy-Efficient Properties

Lenders should give special underwriting consideration to borrowers who are purchasing properties that are energy efficient or that will be undergoing energy-related improvements. Higher monthly housing expense and debt payment ratios may be justified because the borrower will realize savings in energy costs.

The lender should consider the energy savings of a property along with other property and borrower characteristics, when it decides whether increased qualifying ratios are justified. For energy-efficient properties, we allow increases of up to 2% in both the monthly housing expense-to-income ratio and the total obligations-to-income ratio. The property's energy-efficiency must be rated as "high" to justify the use of these increased ratios.

Underwriting an adjustable rate mortgage for a borrower with an energy-efficient home requires additional consideration. By accepting higher ratios, we allow a borrower to commit a greater portion of his or her income to an obligation that has changing payment terms, while reducing his or her ability to adjust budget items for unexpected expenses.

(also see
Section 502.06)

Lenders must retain all energy-related documents that it uses to make the underwriting decision. For each mortgage loan, the lender

Underwriting Guidelines

Special Considerations

Selling

Section 502.01

must have either an *Energy Addendum-Residential Appraisal Report* (FHLMC Form 70A) or evidence that the dwelling was built in accordance with a qualifying energy conservation program. This documentation must be sent to us if we perform a post-purchase review of the mortgage.

Section 502 Special Appraisal Considerations

Some types of properties require special consideration in the appraisal process to recognize the special contributions of unusual features, the detrimental effect of certain environmental conditions, the interrelationship between the property being appraised and other units within the development or project, or the need to meet specific criteria in order for a mortgage on the property to be eligible for delivery to Fannie Mae.

Section 502.01 Units in Cooperative Projects

When an appraiser evaluates a cooperative unit, he or she must estimate the market value of the cooperative interest. The cooperative interest is the ownership interest of the shares that are attributable to the cooperative unit, excluding the unit's *pro rata* share of the blanket mortgage's debt service. In other words, the cooperative interest is the equity portion that is over and above the *pro rata* share of the blanket mortgage(s).

To determine the value of the cooperative interest, the appraiser must include the following information on the *Appraisal Report—Individual Condominium or PUD Unit* (Form 1073), or in an addendum to the appraisal report form:

- The number of shares attributable to the unit;
- The name of the lienholder and the lien position of all project blanket financing;
- The *pro rata* share of the blanket mortgage payments that are attributable to the unit, as determined by dividing the number of the unit's shares by the total number of project shares;
- The *pro rata* share of each lien that is attributable to the unit;
- Any tax abatements or exceptions that are attributable to the unit, and their remaining term and provisions for escalation of real estate taxes. (The dollar amount by which the taxes will increase and the year in which the increase will occur should be shown); and
- Comments about any mechanics' liens that have been filed against the project.

The appraiser must use reliable sources to obtain data on the cooperative project, the individual subject unit, and the comparable properties, and indicate the name of each source on Form 1073 (or

Underwriting Guidelines

Special Considerations

Section 502.01

Selling

on an addendum to it). The appraiser must comment on the adequacy and reasonableness of the cooperative corporation's budget—including the working capital and replacement reserves funds—and address any other factors that could result in the subject unit's monthly debt service increasing. For comparison purposes, the appraiser should indicate in the "sales comparison analysis" adjustment grid the dollar amount of the monthly assessments for each of the comparable sales.

In many areas, there is limited experience with the cooperative form of ownership. Appraisers always must comment on the acceptance of housing cooperatives in the market area. The degree of acceptance is generally reflected in the availability of similar comparable sales data for cooperative units. If there is limited market acceptance of the cooperative form of ownership, or if it is a relatively new form of ownership in the market area, the appraiser must address any effect that has on the marketability and value of the unit that is being appraised. Because Fannie Mae is concerned about the marketability of the subject property, the appraiser must compare the subject unit to the general market area as well as to other units in the subject cooperative project. This comparison should help demonstrate market acceptance of cooperative units in the area. If the appraiser believes that the submission of more than the three required comparable sales is appropriate to support the estimate of market value, he or she should submit other comparable sales—including contracts for sale—as additional supporting data. Comparables must be from similar types of projects—townhouses, mid-rise, high-rise, etc.—that have similar common amenities and recreational facilities.

Generally, when an appraiser appraises a unit in a cooperative project, he or she should use sales of cooperative units as comparables. However, the appraiser may use sales of condominium units as comparables if cooperative unit sales are not available, as long as he or she explains why those types of comparables were used. When there is a preference for condominium ownership in the subject market area, the appraiser must adjust the condominium comparables to reflect the market's reaction to the cooperative unit.

If the subject property is a unit in a new or recently converted cooperative project, the appraiser should select as comparables one closed or settled comparable sale from the subject project (if one is available) and two closed or settled comparable sales from outside of the project. If closed or settled sales are not available in the subject project, the appraiser should use comparable sales from competing projects. When the subject property is a unit in an established cooperative project—one that has resale activity—the appraiser should use as comparables two closed or settled comparable sales from within the subject project (if available) and one closed or settled comparable sale from a competing project.

Underwriting Guidelines

Special Considerations

Selling

Section 502.03

The final adjustment to value must be indicated and explained in the "Reconciliation" section of the appraisal report form. The appraiser must report two values: (1) the unit value, encumbered by the blanket mortgage(s), and (2) the unit value, excluding the unit's *pro rata* share of the blanket mortgage(s). The second value reflects the market value for the unit's cooperative interest. [To illustrate: When the indicated value of the unit encumbered by the blanket mortgage(s) is $100,000 and the unit's *pro rata* share of the blanket mortgage(s) is $25,000, the value estimate for the unit's cooperative interest is $75,000.] The appraiser must certify in the appraisal report that "the *pro rata* share of the blanket mortgage(s) on the real estate has not been included in the market value estimate of the cooperative interest of the unit."

**Section 502.02
Units in
PUD Projects**

A planned unit development (PUD) project is one that consists of common property and improvements that are owned and maintained by an owners' association, corporation, or trust for the benefit and use of the individual units within the project. For a project to qualify as a PUD, the owners' association, corporation, or trust must require automatic, nonseverable membership for each individual unit owner, and provide for mandatory assessments. Zoning should not be the basis for classifying a project as a PUD.

Appraisals for PUD units must be documented on the *Appraisal Report—Individual Condominium or PUD Unit* (Form 1073). The appraisal of an individual unit in a PUD requires the appraiser to analyze the PUD project as well as the individual unit. The appraiser must pay special attention to the location of the project, the location of the individual unit within the project, the project's amenities, and the amount and purpose of the owners' association assessment since the marketability and value of the individual units in a project generally depend on the marketability and appeal of the project itself.

**Section 502.03
Units in Condominium
Projects**

A condominium project is one in which individual owners hold title to units in the project along with an undivided interest in the real estate that is designated as the common area for the project.

Appraisals for condominium units must be documented on the *Appraisal Report—Individual Condominium or PUD Unit* (Form 1073). The appraisal of an individual unit in a condominium project requires the appraiser to analyze the condominium project as well as the individual unit. The appraiser must pay special attention to the location of the project, the location of the individual unit within the project, the project's amenities, and the amount and purpose of the owners' association assessment since the marketability and value of the individual units in a project depend on the marketability and appeal of the project itself.

Underwriting Guidelines

Special Considerations

Section 502.04

Selling

Section 502.04
Manufactured (or Factory-Built) Housing Units

Because we have specific eligibility criteria for mortgages secured by manufactured (or factory-built) housing units, the appraiser should make sure that he or she considers these criteria and adequately addresses them in the appraisal report.

A manufactured housing unit must be legally classified as real estate, must be permanently affixed to a foundation, and must assume the characteristics of site-built housing. It must also have been built under the Federal Home Construction and Safety Standards that were established by HUD in June, 1976. Other factory-built housing—such as prefabricated, panelized, modular, or sectional housing—needs to assume the characteristics of site-built housing and to meet local zoning and building codes.

We do not have minimum requirements for width, size, or roof pitch for manufactured housing units. Each unit must have sufficient square footage and room dimensions to be acceptable to typical purchasers in the subject market area. The wheels, axles, and trailer hitches must be removed when the unit is placed on its permanent site. We require both perimeter and pier foundations to have footings that are located below the frost line. When piers are used, they must be placed where the unit manufacturer recommends. Anchors must be provided if state law requires them. The foundation system must have been designed by an engineer to meet the soil conditions of the site.

The appraiser must address both the marketability and comparability of manufactured housing units. The materials and construction of the improvements must be acceptable in the subject market area. The appraiser should also comment on the sufficiency of the unit's living area, interior room size, storage, adequacy of roof pitch and overhangs, and the compatibility of the exterior finish. In addition, the appraiser must address the marketability and value of manufactured housing units in the subject market area in comparison to the marketability of site-built housing in the area.

Single-width manufactured housing units must be located in a Fannie Mae-approved project; a multi-width unit may be located on an individual lot or in any project (although, in certain areas, our regional office may require subdivision approval for units located on individual lots.)

The appraiser should use as comparable sales similar manufactured housing units—comparing single-width units to single-width units and multi-width units to multi-width units. If comparable sales of similar units are not available, the appraiser may use site-built housing as comparable sales, as long as he or she explains why that

Underwriting Guidelines

Special Considerations

Section 502.06

Selling

is being done. When there is a preference for site-built housing in the subject market area, the appraiser must adjust the site-built comparables to reflect the market's reaction to manufactured housing units.

When the subject property is another kind of factory-built housing, the appraiser should use sales of similar factory-built housing as comparables if they are available. If they are not available, the appraiser may use sales of comparable site-built housing, as long as he or she provides an explanation for doing so and makes appropriate adjustments to reflect any market preferences for site-built housing.

**Section 502.05
Mixed-Use Properties**

Although we will purchase mortgages that are secured by properties that have a business use in addition to their residential use—such as a house in which day care is provided or a professional office—we have special eligibility criteria for them. Therefore, the appraiser should make sure that he or she considers these criteria and adequately addresses them in the appraisal report. Specifically, a mixed-use property

- must be a single-family dwelling;
- must represent a legal, permissible use of the property under the local zoning requirements;
- must not have any special use modifications (or plans for them); and
- must not generate public traffic that could have a possible negative influence on the marketability and value of the subject property.

**Section 502.06
Energy-Efficient
Properties**

When a lender is giving special underwriting consideration to a borrower because the property that secures his or her mortgage is energy efficient, the lender can use either of two methods to qualify the dwelling as energy-efficient: development of an energy-efficiency rating by the appraiser or reliance on the dwelling having been constructed in compliance with qualifying energy conservation programs.

A. Development of appraiser's energy-efficiency rating. This method of determining energy-efficiency can be used for both new construction and existing homes.

The appraiser must include an evaluation of the energy-efficient characteristics and an overall rating—of high, adequate or low—for the dwelling's energy efficiency in the appraisal report. Appraisers

Underwriting Guidelines

Special Considerations

Section 502.06

Selling

may use an *Energy Addendum-Residential Appraisal Report* (FHLMC Form 70A) to develop the rating. Part I of this form, which consists of a checklist and the rating, is used to justify the use of increased ratios in the underwriting process, while Part II is sometimes used to determine the contribution of energy-efficient items to the property's value. A rating of "high" is required to justify consideration in the credit underwriting process. Generally, a dwelling must contain features from each of the following three major categories to receive a "high" rating.

1. *Insulation and Infiltration.* We require insulation with adequate "R" values or infiltration barriers:

- Insulation in ceilings, roofs, or attic floors that are over conditioned spaces, in exterior walls, under floors that cover unheated areas, around slabs, around heating or cooling ducts or pipes that run through unconditioned spaces, around the sill area and around the water heater;

- Caulking or weatherstripping around window and door areas and at the sill area;

- Special fireplace devices or features such as combustion-air and flue dampers, and a fire door;

- Sealing of the sole plate and penetrations of the exterior shell; and

- Dampers for exhaust fans.

2. *Windows and Doors.* We require the following features:

- Double- or triple-pane windows, or storm windows; and

- Storm doors, or insulated doors.

3. *Heating and Cooling Systems.* We require the following types of systems:

- New efficient heating and cooling systems, or appropriate modifications to an existing system:

    — New efficient systems include such things as a high efficiency oil or gas furnace with an Annual Fuel Utilization Efficiency (AFUE) rating of 80% or higher; a high efficiency heat pump with a Seasonal Energy Efficiency Ratio (SEER) measure of 9.0 or greater and a Heating Seasonal Performance Factor (HSPF) of 7.0 or greater; and a central air conditioner with a SEER rating of 9.0 or greater;

    — System modifications include such things as a flame retention oil burner; vent dampers for oil and gas furnaces; pilotless ignition for gas furnaces; and a secondary condensing heat exchanger for gas and oil furnaces;

Selling

Underwriting Guidelines
Special Considerations
Section 502.07

- Zoned heating and/or air conditioning;
- Automatic set-back thermostats; and
- Solar equipment or design.

B. Reliance on qualifying energy conservation programs. This method for qualifying a dwelling as energy-efficient applies to new construction only. Homes that are built in compliance with energy conservation programs that the National Association of Home Builders (NAHB) classifies as meeting the NAHB Thermal Performance Guidelines may be accepted as energy-efficient. In such cases, the *Energy Addendum—Residential Appraisal Report* (FHLMC Form 70A) is not needed to justify higher qualifying ratios, although the appraiser and the lender may find Part II of the form useful in determining the property's value.

Regardless of the method used for qualifying a dwelling as "energy efficient", the appraiser must consider the market's reaction to energy-efficent improvements (or proposed alterations) and reflect their contributory value in the "sales comparison analysis" adjustment grid on the appraisal report form. This adjustment should be based on the appraiser's analysis of comparable properties. However, if adequate comparables are not available, the appraiser may develop an analysis of the present worth of the estimated savings in utility costs. To do this, the appraiser may use a procedure that is similar to the one used in Part II of the *Energy Addendum-Residential Appraisal Report* (FHLMC Form 70A).

**Section 502.07
Environmental Hazards**

If the appraiser has knowledge of any hazardous condition (whether it exists on the subject property or on any site within the immediate vicinity of the property) that affects the value of the subject property —such as the presence of hazardous wastes, toxic substances, asbestos-containing materials, urea-formaldehyde insulation, radon air pollution, etc.—he or she must comment on the hazard's influence on the property's value and marketability and make appropriate adjustments in the overall analysis of the property's value.

22

Home mortgage property appraisal requirements

2201

Appraisal report

The Seller agrees to submit with each mortgage file an appraisal report for the mortgaged premises on the applicable Freddie Mac appraisal form. This appraisal form must be requested by and prepared for the mortgage originator and signed by an appraiser approved by the Seller. Freddie Mac will not accept appraisal reports made for the borrower.

† **(a) Completion of appraisal report.** The appraisal report must be completed in a manner that supports the appraiser's estimate of market value and presents to the reader a visual picture of the neighborhood, site, and improvements. The appraiser is encouraged to use the "Comments" section of the appraisal report or attach addenda to make this presentation. The rating grids must be used to rate the stability and marketability of the mortgaged premises compared with other properties in the mortgaged premises' price range.

(b) Cost approach. The cost approach must include proper adjustments for any items detrimental to stability or marketability, such as physical, functional, and/or external depreciation. Freddie Mac does not consider the cost approach to be appropriate in the appraisal of individual condominium or PUD units. Also, realizing the complexity of estimating depreciation in the evaluation of older 1-4 family properties, Freddie Mac does not rely heavily on the cost approach. The estimated land value must indicate the market value of the land, recognizing its highest and best use.

(c) Sales comparison approach. The value indicated by the sales comparison approach must be supported by an analysis of sales of at least three comparable properties. The comparable properties should have the following characteristics:
- located near the subject property
- recently sold
- closing/settlement has occurred

The analysis must show a description and dollar amount of adjustments for significant variations between the comparable properties and the mortgaged premises.

(d) Income approach. The value indicated by the income approach, if considered applicable by the appraiser, must be derived by the gross rent multiplier technique using market rent. For nonowner-occupied (NOO) investment properties, the appraiser must use the income approach and support the market rent used in the appraisal.

(e) Estimate of market value. The estimate of market value is not based on an average of the values indicated by the three approaches, but on a reconciliation of the soundness of each approach and its applicability to the final estimate of value.

(f) Materials and construction. Freddie Mac does not provide minimum specifications for materials and construction of 1-4 family properties. In reviewing appraisal and inspection reports and in its inspections, Freddie Mac will look for properties whose materials and construction are acceptable to the typical purchaser and to private institutional mortgage investors. Freddie Mac will use the same flexibility in making judgments as such investors use, consistent with the price range of the mortgaged premises.

(g) The residential appraisal report must be dated within 120 days before the date of the note. If the appraisal report is more than 120 days but less than one year old, it must be certified that the property has not declined in value since the date of the original appraisal. The original appraiser or a qualified appraiser approved by the Seller must make such certification.

If the mortgage delivered to Freddie Mac was originated more than one year before the delivery date, the Seller must represent and warrant that as of the delivery date the market value of the mortgaged premises is at least equal to its appraised value as of the origination date of the mortgage. For such mortgages, Freddie Mac will not require a new appraisal.

(h) Adverse environmental influences. The appraiser must comment on the effect of any observable environmental influences or conditions which may adversely affect
- the value of the property or
- the health of the mortgaged premises' inhabitants

Such environmental influences or conditions may include, but are not limited to
- any presence of asbestos, urea-formaldehyde foam, or similar insulation in dwelling
- proximity of the mortgaged premises to industrial sites, waste or water treatment facilities, or commercial establishments which use or store chemicals or oil products in their operations (e.g., gasoline stations, dry cleaners)

The appraiser must carefully consider any detected influences, make any appropriate adjustments to market value, and comment on the effect of detected influences or conditions on the marketability of the mortgaged premises.

† **(i) Subsidence.** The appraiser must note the presence (observable or known) of any areas of subsidence or other significant earth movements within the subject site and surrounding neighborhood. Such areas of subsidence or earth movement may include, but are not limited to, noticeable depressions in the subject site, sink holes, abnormal settling of the improvements, land slides, collapsed underground mines, and earth faults. In addition, the appraiser must consider the effect of such presence in estimating the subject property's market value and any effect on marketability.

2202

Appraisal forms: single-family properties

The Uniform Residential Appraisal Report (Form 70, exhibit 15), dated 10/86, must be used for all appraisals of single-family properties and deminimis PUD units dated on or after May 1, 1987. Appraisals of single family properties or deminimis PUD units dated before May 1, 1987, must be on either Form 70 or on the appraisal form approved by Freddie Mac for use at that time.

For appraisals of deminimis PUD units dated after June 30, 1987, the appraiser must describe the development's common property in the additional features portion of the comments section on Form 70. The information contained in the appraisal report must not contradict the Seller's determination that the project is a deminimis PUD as defined in section 0207.

2203

Appraisal forms: two-family properties

The Appraisal Report—Small Residential Income Property (Form 72, exhibit 19), dated 7/79, or the Form 70 approved by Freddie Mac for use at that time must be used for all appraisals of two-family properties, including those in a deminimis PUD, dated on or after January 1, 1980. Appraisals of two-family properties dated before January 1, 1980, must be on Form 72 or Form 70 approved by Freddie Mac for use at that time.

2204

Appraisal forms: three- or four-family properties

Either the Appraisal Report—Small Residential Income Property (Form 72, exhibit 19), dated 7/79, or the Appraisal Report—Residential Income Property (Form 71B, exhibit 18) must be used for all appraisals of three- or four-family properties (including those in a deminimis PUD) dated on or after November 1, 1979. Appraisals of three- to four-family properties dated before November 1, 1979, may be on either of these forms or on the Form 70 approved by Freddie Mac for use at that time.

2205

Appraisal forms: condominium or PUD units (except deminimis PUD units)

The Appraisal Report—Individual Condominium or PUD Unit (Form 465, exhibit 30), must be used for all appraisals of condominium units (Classes I, II, and III) and PUD units (Classes I, II, and III) dated on or after January 1, 1981. Addendum A to Form 465 must be included if less than 70 percent of the units in the project have been sold to bona fide purchasers. Addendum B to Form 465 (front only) must be included if the developer control has not terminated or if the homeowners association has not been controlled by the unit owners for two or more years. Freddie Mac does not require the reverse side of Addendum B. Condominium and PUD appraisals dated before January 1, 1981, may be on Form 465 or on the appraisal form approved by Freddie Mac for use at that time.

2206

Special flood hazard area designation

The site section of all Freddie Mac single-family appraisal forms asks if the property is located within a FEMA Flood Hazard Area. This question must be answered in the space provided on the form, and if answered "Yes," the FEMA Flood Zone indicated.

2207

Satisfactory completion certificate

For appraisals made subject to repairs, alterations, or conditions, or subject to completion per plans and specifications, the Seller agrees to submit a satisfactory completion certificate to Freddie Mac on the delivery date (unless an escrow account has been established in accordance with section 1202 or 1306). (See Form 442, exhibit 26, for a suggested format for the completion certificate.) This report must be made after completion of repairs, improvements, alterations, conditions, or construction, and must clearly state compliance with all conditions or requirements as stated in the original appraisal report of the mortgaged premises. This report should be prepared by the original appraiser, if possible.

For appraisals reflecting evidence of dampness, infestation, or abnormal settlement, the Seller agrees to submit evidence of corrective action (e.g., an exterminator's certificate or an engineer's report) to Freddie Mac on the delivery date. If corrective action was not a condition of the appraisal, the appraiser must have commented on the effects of the adverse conditions on value and marketability.

2208

Construction warranty program

If the single family home, condominium, or PUD is covered by a warranty program, the appraiser should describe the program in the space provided in the appraisal report.

2209

Zoning restrictions, code requirements†

The mortgaged premises must conform to all applicable zoning and use restrictions and enable the mortgage to qualify as a "home mortgage" as defined in section 0212.

Freddie Mac may, however, purchase a home mortgage secured by a 1-4 family property that does not conform to applicable zoning and use restrictions but is a "legal use" (known as "legal nonconforming use"). The appraiser must comment on any adverse effect of any nonconforming usage when estimating the market value and marketability of the property.

Freddie Mac's policy on legal nonconforming condominium projects is found in section 2001.

2210

Residential property†

Freddie Mac's statutory purpose is to purchase residential mortgages; it does not purchase mortgages secured by vacant land or property used primarily for agriculture, farming, or commercial enterprise. Factors to be considered in determining that a property is residential in purpose include, but are not limited to,
- the type of improvements on the subject property and neighboring properties
- the current use of the subject property and neighboring properties
- the degree, amount, and type of development occurring in the area
- pending zoning changes or changes in use of properties in the area

Generally, Freddie Mac will not purchase a mortgage secured on a property located in an area built up less than 25 percent if the land value of the subject property exceeds 30 percent of the total property value unless it is demonstrated that
- the subject property and neighboring properties are residential in nature and marketable and
- the land size and land value-to-total value ratio are typical

2211

Section 2211 is deleted.

2212

Discontinuance of an appraiser by Freddie Mac

Freddie Mac may at any time refuse to accept appraisals made by specific appraisers or notify the Seller that it will no longer accept appraisals made by a given appraiser. Thereafter, the Seller must not use that appraiser for mortgages purchased by Freddie Mac.

2213

Representations to third parties by appraiser

Freddie Mac does not approve appraisers but accepts appraisals made by appraisers who are approved by the Seller. An appraiser must not make any representation to third parties as being approved and qualified by Freddie Mac.

2214

Energy efficient properties

An energy efficient property uses cost effective design, materials, equipment, and site orientation to conserve nonrenewable fuels. Implicit in this definition are proper design and installation of materials and equipment consistent with the climate in the area. Items that contribute to the energy efficiency of a property include, but are not limited to, the following:
- insulation with adequate R-values installed in ceilings, exterior walls, and roofs; around hot water heaters; under floors that cover unheated areas; and surrounding ducts and pipes in unconditioned areas
- caulking and weatherstripping

- double or triple pane windows
- window shading or landscaping for solar control
- storm fittings
- automatic setback thermostats
- heating, cooling, and lighting systems and appliances designed to be energy efficient
- solar systems for water heating, space heating, and cooling
- wood-fired heating systems
- building designs that minimize energy use, such as smaller window area and earth sheltering

† The appraiser should list any energy efficient items in the appraisal report, and note the amount of their contribution to value in the "Sales Comparison Analysis" section. The appraiser should comment on the adequacy of insulation in the report. Energy efficient items indicated on the appraisal report should be noted by the Seller for their potential energy savings and possible addition to value. At the Seller's option, the Energy Addendum—Residential Appraisal Report (Form 70A) or, an established home energy rating system (HERS) sponsored by a local utility, home builder association, or a state or local government may be used to identify, rate, and evaluate the property's energy-related features. The Seller should give special consideration to these items since an energy efficient property could affect credit underwriting guidelines.

2215

Market value

Market value is defined in the following manner: "the most probable price which a property should bring in a competitive and open market under all conditions requisite to a fair sale, the buyer and seller, each acting prudently, knowledgeably and assuming the price is not affected by undue stimulus. Implicit in this definition is the consummation of a sale as of a specified date and the passing of title from seller to buyer under conditions whereby: (1) buyer and seller are typically motivated; (2) both parties are well informed or well advised, and each acting in what he considers his own best interest; (3) a reasonable time is allowed for exposure in the open market; (4) payment is made in terms of cash in U.S. dollars or in terms of financial arrangements comparable thereto; and (5) the price represents the normal consideration for the property sold unaffected by special or creative financing or sales concessions* granted by anyone associated with the sale.

*Adjustments to the comparables must be made for special or creative financing or sales concessions. No adjustments are necessary for those costs which are normally paid by sellers as a result of tradition or law in a market area; these costs are readily identifiable since the seller pays these costs in virtually all sales transactions. Special or creative financing adjustments can be made to the comparable property by comparisons to financing terms offered by a third-party institutional lender that is not already involved in the property or transaction. Any adjustment should not be calculated on a mechanical dollar-for-dollar cost of the financing or concession but the dollar amount of any adjustment should approximate the market's reaction to the financing or concessions based on the appraiser's judgment."

Note: In evaluation of properties, Freddie Mac will not consider value assigned to furniture or any other personal property.

2216

Discrimination in appraising

The appraiser must certify that the estimate of market value in the appraisal report is not based in whole or in part on the race, color, sex, marital status, religion, or national origin of the prospective owners or occupants of the property appraised, or on the race, color, or national origin of the present owners or occupants of the properties in the vicinity of the property appraised. (See section 0502.)

As a matter of corporate policy, Freddie Mac will reject any loan supported by an appraisal report that makes reference to race or the racial composition of the neighborhood.

2217

Property inspections: 1–4 family properties

In addition to reviewing the documents submitted by the Seller, Freddie Mac will make property inspections and other checks to assure proper underwriting of the mortgages offered for sale to Freddie Mac.

2218

Property inspections: condominium or PUD properties

Before purchasing the initial mortgage from a Class I condominium or PUD project, Freddie Mac must inspect the project. If the project is being constructed in sections/phases, Freddie Mac must inspect each section/phase.

If requested by the Seller, Freddie Mac will inspect a project before the delivery date under the existing project approval program or early project approval program.

Existing project approval program. A project will be inspected under the existing project approval program if
- the condominium or PUD has been created and is existing in full compliance with all the requirements and applicable laws of the jurisdiction where the condominium or PUD is located;
- the improvements, including amenities, have been completed sufficiently to allow analysis of the physical characteristics of the project and individual units;
- sufficient sales have been made to indicate its marketability.

An inspection will relate only to the physical characteristics, location, and marketability of the project, not to the acceptability of the condominium/PUD constituent documents, individual mortgage loan applications, or mortgage instruments. The inspection does not constitute Freddie Mac's endorsement of the project. After the inspection has been completed, the Seller will be advised by a letter stating conditions of approval or rejection of the project. This advice does not constitute prior approval of any mortgage, an agreement by Freddie Mac to purchase any mortgage, or a waiver of any warranties required in this guide.

Freddie Mac will require the Seller to pay an inspection fee if the Seller requests an inspection of an existing project; and if the Seller requests a waiver and/or modification of agreements, representations, warranties, or a classification as a deminimis PUD, that necessitates an inspection. The inspection fee for each project or section/phase is $500, plus $10 per unit for each unit in excess of 50 units, with a maximum charge of $2,000 per inspection. This fee is nonrefundable and must be paid before the inspection. Only one inspection fee will be charged if condominium or PUD mortgages to be delivered under different types of purchase contracts are within the same project or section/phase or if two or more sections/phases are completed at the time of the inspection.

†**Early project approval program.** A project will be inspected under the early project approval program if the project does not meet the requirements for inspection under the existing project approval program.

Freddie Mac will inspect the property upon receipt of a complete submission package as specified in section 2219. If the property and all exhibits are acceptable, Freddie Mac will issue a Conditional Project Approval (Form 772, exhibit 50). This conditional approval will be subject to the completion of construction, presale and owner-occupancy requirements, and other conditions and requirements indicated on the conditional project approval. Conditional project approvals are not for the exclusive benefit of any one Seller; however, documentation to satisfy the conditions and requirements must be submitted by one Seller at one time. After the conditions and requirements are met by the Seller, to Freddie Mac's satisfaction, Freddie Mac will advise the Seller in writing, of project approval.

An inspection will relate only to Freddie Mac's assessment of existing physical characteristics. The inspection, the conditional project approval, or final project approval do not constitute an endorsement of the project, approval of constituent documents, or prior approval of any unit mortgages by Freddie Mac. Also, issuance of conditional project approvals are not waivers of the *Sellers' and Servicers' Guide* requirements or warranties. Any fees for waiver of any *Sellers' and Servicers' Guide* requirements are the same as in the existing project approval program.

Conditional project approvals are issued for periods of up to two years. Requests for extensions of conditional project approvals will be considered by Freddie Mac upon receipt of project status updates and a statement of reasons for the request. If the Seller requests an extension of the approval that in Freddie Mac's judgement requires an inspection, the Seller must pay Freddie Mac an extension fee of $500.

2219

Property inspections: project documentation for Class I condo or PUD projects.

Initial mortgage or existing project documentation. With the submission of the initial mortgage from a Class I condominium or PUD project, or under the existing project approval program, the Seller must submit the following documentation:

- Form 465 including addenda A and B, Appraisal Report—Individual Condominium or PUD Unit (exhibit 30), and if a prior inspection request, a separate report for each different type of unit (See section 2205.)
- a plat of survey, plat map, or a reasonable facsimile, such as a hand drawing, showing the location of improvements and common elements on the site
- a location map, identifying the subject property and each comparable property
- sufficient photographs of the subject property, clearly showing typical buildings, all common elements, recreational amenities, and neighboring improvements. These photographs must be originals, preferably in color, and attached to separate sheets of paper.
- if a prior inspection request, floor plans or sketches, with approximated dimensions of each model type
- if the improvements are in legal but nonconforming use relative to zoning, documentation from the appropriate regulatory authority outlining the conditions under which and to what extent reconstruction is permitted, if damage to the units or common elements occurs
- if individual units are on leasehold estates, Form 461, Ground Lease Analysis (exhibit 29), for the lease instruments or proposed lease instruments
- a certification (and waiver request, if any) complying with the provisions in section 2002 or 2102, or if a prior inspection request, a letter stating the Seller's ability to submit the certification and describing any waiver request probable when the initial mortgage from that project is delivered to Freddie Mac for purchase. Each certification and letter must be signed by an authorized officer of the Seller.
- a cover letter from the Seller, providing any other information the Seller deems necessary
- if the project is a conversion, additional documentation as indicated in section 2220

Freddie Mac may request additional information or documentation on any project.

Early Project Approval documentation. The Seller must submit the following documentation for consideration under the early project approval program:

- a completed Request for Early Project Approval (Form 770, exhibit 48);
- the Early Project Approval Exhibit Checklist (Form 771, exhibit 49);

- a nonrefundable application fee of $1,000 made payable to the Federal Home Loan Mortgage Corporation drawn on the Seller's account;
- a completed Form 465, Appraisal Report—Individual Condominium or PUD Unit (exhibit 30) for each basic unit type; dated within 90 days of the request for early project approval;
- a completed Addendum A to Form 465, Project Analysis, (exhibit 30) on each phase/section or on the entire project if not developed according to phases/sections;
- a completed Addendum B to Form 465, Analysis of Annual Income and Expense, on each phase/section or on the entire project if not developed according to phases/sections and on each applicable master/umbrella homeowner association. Seller must execute the certificate at the bottom of page 1 of Addendum B;
- the survey or site plan for the total project delineating each phase, and showing the actual and/or proposed location of all improvements, easements, and common elements on the site.
- a location map identifying the location of the subject property and each comparable property;
- photographs of the site clearly showing major access, street scenes adjacent to the site, and neighborhood improvements. Photographs of comparable property sales must also be submitted and properly identified (all photographs must be originals, preferably in color, and attached to a separate sheet of paper). If models or amenities are completed, photographs of these items are to be submitted. Photographs of all existing improvements should be included;
- floor plans of each different type of unit with dimensions and elevation plans of every type of structure;
- descriptions of any potential levy of public and private assessments for improvements (whether on-site or off-site), whether such assessments can be prepaid and proposed method of payment;
- descriptions of any easements (other than those for which title exception waivers are not required) and road maintenance agreements;
- if the improvements are in legal but nonconfirming use relative to current zoning regulations, documentation from the appropriate regulatory authority, outlining the conditions under which and to what extent reconstruction is permitted, if damage to the units or common elements occur;
- if individual units in the condominium or PUD project are on leasehold estates, a completed Ground Lease Analysis (Form 461, exhibit 29);
- if the project is a conversion, additional documentation as required in section 2220.

Freddie Mac may request additional information or documentation on any project.

2220

Property inspections: additional documentation for condominium conversion

If the project is a condominium conversion, the following documentation must also be included:
- licensed engineer's report indicating the structural integrity of the building and the condition of the major systems, including the heating, cooling, plumbing, and electrical systems, and the roof and elevators. If the engineer's report indicates any deficiencies, the Seller must indicate in the "Description of the Renovation and Rehabilitation" section the actions the sponsor or developer has taken or will take to cure the deficiencies.
- description of the renovation and rehabilitation proposed or in process
- the income and expense statements for the rental project covering the two-year period before conversion, and a schedule of the preconversion rents received for each major model type

Freddie Mac may request additional information or documentation on any project.

2221

Appraisers

Freddie Mac does not approve specific appraisers. Appraisers are approved and selected by the loan originator and confirmed by the Seller by warranty. An appraisal delivered to Freddie Mac is deemed to be the Seller's representation as to the professional quality of the appraisal and estimate of market value. The Seller is expected to review each appraisal in detail for its completeness, accuracy, and appraising logic. Appraisals found to be deficient will be considered a breach of the Seller's warranty as to the security of the mortgage and the purchase documents, and such violation will subject the Seller to the sanctions available to Freddie Mac.

The appraiser must be experienced in the appraisal of properties similar to the type being appraised and be actively engaged in appraisal work. In addition, the appraiser should
- have successfully completed courses in real estate appraisal,
- have a knowledge of current real estate market conditions and financing trends in the subject area,
- have a working knowledge of construction costs, materials, methods, and standards in the area, and
- maintain a file on real estate sale transactions, including the financing involved.

Freddie Mac reserves the right, in its sole discretion, to refuse to accept appraisals made by specific appraisers.

2222

Certification statement of limiting conditions†

The Seller must have on file, or have attached to each appraisal report submitted to Freddie Mac, Form 439, Certification and Statement of Limiting Conditions (exhibit 25), executed by the appraiser.

Freddie Mac's
Single-Family Appraisal Form 70

Appraisal must be requested and prepared for the mortgage originator and signed by an appraiser approved by the seller.

Appraisal should be filled out completely and written in an objective manner so that a third party can follow appraiser's reasoning in arriving at the estimate of market value.

SUBJECT								
Property Address				Census Tract		LENDER DISCRETIONARY USE		
City		County	State	Zip Code		Sale Price	$	
Legal Description						Date		
Owner/Occupant				Map Reference		Mortgage Amount	$	
Sale Price $		Date of Sale		PROPERTY RIGHTS APPRAISED		Mortgage Type		
Loan charges/concessions to be paid by seller $				☐ Fee Simple		Discount Points and Other Concessions		
R.E. Taxes $		Tax Year	HOA $/Mo.	☐ Leasehold		Paid by Seller	$	
Lender/Client				☐ Condominium (HUD/VA)				
				☐ De Minimis PUD		Source		

NEIGHBORHOOD										
LOCATION	☐ Urban	☐ Suburban	☐ Rural	NEIGHBORHOOD ANALYSIS		Good	Avg.	Fair	Poor
BUILT UP	☐ Over 75%	☐ 25-75%	☐ Under 25%	Employment Stability		☐	☐	☐	☐
GROWTH RATE	☐ Rapid	☐ Stable	☐ Slow	Convenience to Employment		☐	☐	☐	☐
PROPERTY VALUES	☐ Increasing	☐ Stable	☐ Declining	Convenience to Shopping		☐	☐	☐	☐
DEMAND/SUPPLY	☐ Shortage	☐ In Balance	☐ Over Supply	Convenience to Schools		☐	☐	☐	☐
MARKETING TIME	☐ Under 3 Mos.	☐ 3-6 Mos.	☐ Over 6 Mos.	Adequacy of Public Transportation		☐	☐	☐	☐
PRESENT LAND USE %	LAND USE CHANGE	PREDOMINANT	SINGLE FAMILY HOUSING	Recreation Facilities		☐	☐	☐	☐
Single Family ___	Not Likely ☐	OCCUPANCY	PRICE AGE	Adequacy of Utilities		☐	☐	☐	☐
2-4 Family ___	Likely ☐	Owner ☐	$ (000) (yrs)	Property Compatibility		☐	☐	☐	☐
Multi-family ___	In process ☐	Tenant ☐	Low	Protection from Detrimental Cond.		☐	☐	☐	☐
Commercial ___	To:	Vacant (0-5%) ☐	High	Police & Fire Protection		☐	☐	☐	☐
Industrial ___		Vacant (over 5%) ☐	Predominant	General Appearance of Properties		☐	☐	☐	☐
Vacant ___			—	Appeal to Market		☐	☐	☐	☐

Note: Race or the racial composition of the neighborhood are not considered reliable appraisal factors.
COMMENTS: _____

SUBJECT: Should be filled out completely and verified by reviewing tax bills, plats of survey and other recognized real estate records and source books.

NEIGHBORHOOD: Should be complete and accurate, location is critical to value.

LOCATION/DEVELOPMENT: Residential, market acceptance.

GROWTH/VALUES TREND/SUPPLY & DEMAND: If slow, declining or over-supplied, determine whether just subject neighborhood or area-wide. Have prices bottomed out? Comment on the effect on marketability.

MARKETING TIME: Comment on effect on marketability if over six months.

PRESENT LAND USE: Successful mix.

CHANGE IN PRESENT LAND USE: Effect on marketability.

OWNER OCCUPANCY/VACANCIES: Effect on marketability.

PRICE RANGE: Exceeds, is it acceptable to typical buyer? Below, are improvements in at least average condition?

RATING GRID: Subject neighborhoods rated against competing neighborhoods. Characteristics important to typical buyer, all fair or poor ratings should be satisfactorily explained.

Freddie Mac will reject any loan supported by an appraisal report which makes reference to race.

Dimensions						Topography
Site Area			Corner Lot			Size
Zoning Classification			Zoning Compliance			Shape
HIGHEST & BEST USE: Present Use			Other Use			Drainage
UTILITIES	Public	Other	SITE IMPROVEMENTS Type	Public	Private	View
Electricity	☐		Street	☐	☐	Landscaping
Gas	☐		Curb/Gutter	☐	☐	Driveway
Water	☐		Sidewalk	☐	☐	Apparent Easements
Sanitary Sewer	☐		Street Lights	☐	☐	FEMA Flood Hazard Yes* No
Storm Sewer	☐		Alley	☐	☐	FEMA* Map/Zone

COMMENTS (Apparent adverse easements, encroachments, special assessments, slide areas, etc.):

SITE: Size, shape & topography should be generally acceptable to the market—steep lot or flat lot should have comments about excess erosion or drainage.

ZONING: Subject property should conform to zoning requirements. However, Freddie Mac may purchase a home mortgage secured by property that does not conform to applicable zoning and use restrictions but is a "Legal Use" (legal non-conforming). Appraiser must comment on any adverse effect on any non-conforming usage when estimating the market value and marketability of the property.

HIGHEST & BEST USE: If other than subject use, explain.

UTILITIES: Must meet community standards.

SITE IMPROVEMENTS: Must meet community standards. Use of private street must be legally enforceable. Charges for maintenance of private streets must be included in underwriting ratios.

IMPROVEMENTS	GENERAL DESCRIPTION	EXTERIOR DESCRIPTION	FOUNDATION	BASEMENT	INSULATION
	Units	Foundation	Slab	Area Sq. Ft.	Roof
	Stories	Exterior Walls	Crawl Space	% Finished	Ceiling
	Type (Det./Att.)	Roof Surface	Basement	Ceiling	Walls
	Design (Style)	Gutters & Dwnspts.	Sump Pump	Walls	Floor
	Existing	Window Type	Dampness	Floor	None
	Proposed	Storm Sash	Settlement	Outside Entry	Adequacy
	Under Construction	Screens	Infestation		Energy Efficient Items:
	Age (Yrs.)	Manufactured House			
	Effective Age (Yrs.)				

ROOMS	Foyer	Living	Dining	Kitchen	Den	Family Rm.	Rec. Rm.	Bedrooms	# Baths	Laundry	Other	Area Sq. Ft.
Basement												
Level 1												
Level 2												

Finished area **above** grade contains: _____ Rooms; _____ Bedroom(s); _____ Bath(s); _____ Square Feet of Gross Living Area

SURFACES	Materials/Condition	HEATING		KITCHEN EQUIP.		ATTIC		IMPROVEMENT ANALYSIS	Good	Avg	Fair	Poor
Floors		Type		Refrigerator		None		Quality of Construction				
Walls		Fuel		Range/Oven		Stairs		Condition of Improvements				
Trim/Finish		Condition		Disposal		Drop Stair		Room Sizes/Layout				
Bath Floor		Adequacy		Dishwasher		Scuttle		Closets and Storage				
Bath Wainscot		COOLING		Fan/Hood		Floor		Energy Efficiency				
Doors		Central		Compactor		Heated		Plumbing-Adequacy & Condition				
		Other		Washer/Dryer		Finished		Electrical-Adequacy & Condition				
		Condition		Microwave				Kitchen Cabinets-Adequacy & Cond.				
Fireplace(s)	#	Adequacy		Intercom				Compatibility to Neighborhood				

CAR STORAGE:	Garage		Attached		Adequate		House Entry		Appeal & Marketability				
No. Cars	Carport		Detached		Inadequate		Outside Entry		Estimated Remaining Economic Life				Yrs.
Condition	None		Built-In		Electric Door		Basement Entry		Estimated Remaining Physical Life				Yrs.

Additional features: _____

Depreciation (Physical, functional and external inadequacies, repairs needed, modernization, etc.): _____

General market conditions and prevalence and impact in subject/market area regarding loan discounts, interest buydowns and concessions _____

FEMA FLOOD HAZARD: If property is located in flood zone, must be checked "yes" and FEMA map/zone must be listed. Freddie Mac will not purchase mortgages secured by properties where the improvements are located in a flood hazard zone without adequate flood hazard insurance.

IMPROVEMENTS: No minimum specifications for material and construction. Must be typical of the area.

FOUNDATION: When evidence of dampness, settlement or infestation is present, verification that corrective action has been taken or comments on the effect on the marketability are required.

ROOM LIST: Floor plan should appeal to typical buyer for market. Any functional obsolescence should be noted and/or adjusted for.

INTERIOR: Should be consistent with typical buyer's expectations.

IMPROVEMENT ANALYSIS: Subject property improvements rated against comparable properties in subject neighborhood. Any fair or poor ratings must be satisfactorily explained.

Comment section should be used to describe any repairs needed, functional inadequacies observed, positive or negative characteristics of the property as well as impact on market area regarding loan discounts, interest buydowns and concessions.

Structures with conversions or additions that lack permits are acceptable only under these conditions:

- No value given to the square footage.
- Appraiser considers "Cost-to-Cure" if applicable, to arrive at value.
- No credit given for rents or income derived from un-permitted additions.
- Seller warrants marketability of property. If property becomes REO and market value or saleability is impaired, repurchase will be required for violation of S/S guide section 2209.

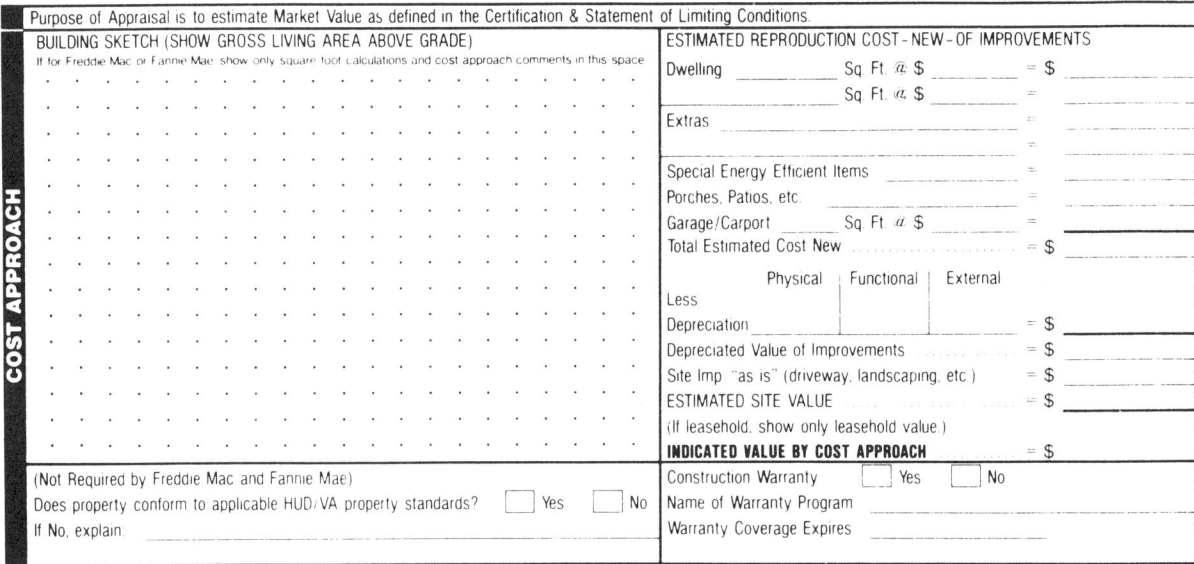

COST APPROACH

- **Freddie Mac prefers to see cost approach. If not applicable, we must at least have "estimated site value".**
- **Must include adjustments for items adversely affecting marketability such as physical, functional and/or external depreciation as well as explanations thereof.**

RESIDENTIAL PROPERTY: Freddie Mac's statutory purpose is to purchase residential mortgages; it does not purchase mortgages secured by vacant land or property used primarily for agriculture, farming, or commercial enterprise. Factors to be considered in determining that a property is residential in purpose include, but are not limited to:

- The type of improvements on the subject property and neighboring properties.
- The current use of the subject property and neighboring properties.
- The degree, amount, and type of development occurring in the area.

Generally, Freddie Mac will not purchase a mortgage secured on a property located in an area built up less than 25 percent if the land value of the subject property exceeds 30 percent of the total property value unless it is demonstrated that:

- The subject property and neighboring properties are residential in nature and marketable, and
- The land size and land value-to-total value ratio are typical.

The undersigned has recited three recent sales of properties most similar and proximate to subject and has considered these in the market analysis. The description includes a dollar adjustment, reflecting market reaction to those items of significant variation between the subject and comparable properties. If a significant item in the comparable property is superior to, or more favorable than, the subject property, a minus (−) adjustment is made, thus reducing the indicated value of subject; if a significant item in the comparable is inferior to, or less favorable than, the subject property, a plus (+) adjustment is made, thus increasing the indicated value of the subject.				
ITEM	SUBJECT	COMPARABLE NO. 1	COMPARABLE NO. 2	COMPARABLE NO. 3
Address				
Proximity to Subject				
Sales Price	$	$	$	$
Price/Gross Liv. Area	$	$	$	$
Data Source				
VALUE ADJUSTMENTS	DESCRIPTION	DESCRIPTION + (−) $ Adjustment	DESCRIPTION + (−) $ Adjustment	DESCRIPTION + (−) $ Adjustment
Sales or Financing Concessions				
Date of Sale/Time				
Location				
Site/View				
Design and Appeal				
Quality of Construction				
Age				
Condition				
Above Grade Room Count	Total / Bdrms / Baths	Total / Bdrms / Baths	Total / Bdrms / Baths	Total / Bdrms / Baths
Gross Living Area	Sq. Ft.	Sq. Ft.	Sq. Ft.	Sq. Ft.
Basement & Finished Rooms Below Grade				
Functional Utility				
Heating/Cooling				
Garage/Carport				
Porches, Patio, Pools, etc.				
Special Energy Efficient Items				
Fireplace(s)				
Other (e.g. kitchen equip., remodeling)				
Net Adj. (total)		□ + □ − $	□ + □ − $	□ + □ − $
Indicated Value of Subject		$	$	$
Comments on Sales Comparison:				

SALES COMPARISON ANALYSIS

PROXIMITY: Within reasonable proximity to demonstrate similar market conditions.

DATA SOURCE: Unbiased, verifiable and commonly acceptable to area—must be closed sales.

SALES/FINANCING CONCESSIONS: Adjust to reflect what a typical buyer would pay without concessions.

LOCATION, SITE/VIEW, DESIGN & APPEAL, QUALITY OF CONSTRUCTION, AGE, CONDITION, ROOM COUNT, GROSS LIVING AREA, BASEMENT, UTILITY, HEATING/COOLING, GARAGE/ PARKING, PORCHES/PATIOS, ENERGY ITEMS, FIREPLACES & OTHER

- All adjustments should reflect what typical buyers in the marketplace are paying for certain elements. Such adjustments should not necessarily represent preselected cost data.

- Significant adjustments for location, site/view, design/appeal and quality of construction should be explained in comment section.

Suggested guidelines for maximum adjustments are 10% per line and 15% gross adjustment. Where insufficient market data is available, explain reasoning for comparables chosen and address impact on realiability of value.

INCOME APPROACH: Required on all non-owner occupied investment properties. Appraiser must support market rent by either actual rents or survey.

If appraisal made "subject to", a completed Form 442 "satisfactory completion certificate" signed by the original appraiser, if possible, must be obtained and retained in file prior to sale to Freddie Mac.

ESTIMATE OF MARKET VALUE

The final value should be a single value, not a range. The appraiser must be able to support and defend his conclusions; he must be able to support his case for the ultimate value given.

SELLER/SERVICER GUIDE, VOLUME 1, CHAPTER 2201

Appraisal must be prepared in accordance with R-41c. (Per FHLB Memo A B 80, dated 2/26/87, regarding R-41c clarification:

"Compliance with Freddie Mac and Fannie Mae appraisal and appraisal reporting guidelines (and standard form reports) is sufficient for appraisals on existing one-to-four family dwellings and multi-family properties."

- Appraisals must be dated within 120 days from the date of the note.

- Appraisals over 120 days old but less than one year can be recertified by original appraiser or a qualified appraiser approved by the seller.
- If subject mortgage originated more than one year prior to sale to Freddie Mac, seller warrants market value has not declined.

ATTACHMENTS/EXHIBITS

- Provide plan sketch of building and related improvements with exterior dimensions.
- Provide photographs showing subject's front and rear views and street scenes as well as photos of comparable whenever possible.

HUD/FHA Guidelines

EXHIBIT I

INSTRUCTIONS FOR COMPLETING THE UNIFORM RESIDENTIAL APPRAISAL REPORT (URAR)

The URAR should present no difficulty to most appraisers; however, certain areas require instructions to assure proper completion. These areas are identified below. You are reminded that the requirement for photographs remains unchanged.

FHA CASE NUMBER: To be inserted at top right after "File No."

SUBJECT: To be filled in by the appraiser except for the box at right "Lender Discretionary Use" which is to be completed by the field office or direct endorsement lender's underwriter after the purchaser has been approved and the case is ready for closing.

NEIGHBORHOOD: Location: In addition to checking boxes in "predominant occupancy", show percentage occupied. When boxes "urban" and "declining" are both checked, the appraiser should consider making a recommendation that the mortgage encumbering the property be insured pursuant to Section 223(e).

NEIGHBORHOOD ANALYSIS: Mark the most appropriate rating for each item.

G - GOOD:	The item or characteristic in the subject neighborhood is *superior* to the same characteristic found in a competing neighborhood.
A - AVERAGE:	The item or characteristic is *equal* to the same characteristic found in a competing neighborhood.
F - FAIR:	The item or characteristic is *below* the same characteristic found in a competing neighborhood.
P - POOR:	The item or characteristic is in *small supply* or does not exist in the subject neighborhood but is found in a competing neighborhood.

SITE:

DIMENSIONS: List all dimensions of the site. If irregular, the appraiser should show boundary dimensions, such as 85'x150'x195'x250'.

SITE AREA: Enter area in square feet or acres.

CORNER LOT: Enter "Yes" or "No."

ZONING CLASSIFICATION: Enter the zoning type used by the local municipality to describe the type of use permitted. Do not use abbreviations such as "R1" or "A1" by themselves. The abbreviated descriptions can vary among communities. For example:

"residential - single family"
"residential - 1-4 family"

Can use "Historic," if applicable.

If a nonconforming use exists, enter "nonconforming" and state whether it is a legal use which has been approved by the local zoning authority. Be sure to determine if current use is in compliance.

ZONING COMPLIANCE: Enter "yes" or "No/legal nonconforming use." A nonconforming use could require an Addendum for further explanation.

HIGHEST AND BEST USE: PRESENT USE: This entry represents the highest and best use of the site in relation to the neighborhood.

If present use represents the highest and best use, enter "Yes." If it does not, enter "No" and explain in the "Comments" section.

OTHER USE: If the present use is not the highest and best use of the site, enter the use that should exist and explain in the "Comments" section.

UTILITIES: Either check a box or explain under "Other". Public utilities are provided by a government. "Other" can reflect individual and/or community systems. Show if electricity is underground.

SITE IMPROVEMENTS: Describe by entering either "Yes" or "No" and/or a brief description under "Type" and checking whether Public or Private. For example: "Street - Asphalt; Public." It is important to identify if year-round maintenance exists. "Public" refers to a government which can regulate use. It does not include a homeowners association.

TOPOGRAPHY: Enter whether level, sloped, etc.

SIZE: Enter descriptions such as "typical," "small," or "large."

SHAPE: Enter site configuration, such as "triangular," "square," or "rectangular."

DRAINAGE: Enter whether adequate or inadequate. If inadequate, be sure to explain and make requirements for correction, if feasible.

VIEW: Describe briefly the view from the property. Identify a view having a significant positive or negative influence on the value, for example:
"mountains - (and enter "average," "superior" or "inferior" as contrasted with other local sites)
"ocean"
"expressway"

LANDSCAPING: Enter whether adequate or inadequate relative to neighborhood.

DRIVEWAY: Enter type such as concrete, asphalt or gravel.

APPARENT EASEMENTS: If there appears to be an easement, check to make sure.

FEMA FLOOD HAZARD: FEMA is the Federal Emergency Management Agency, which is responsible for mapping flood hazard areas. If any part of the property is inside a Special Flood Hazard area, check "Yes." Otherwise check "No."

FEMA MAP/ZONE: If you have checked the previous question "Yes" enter map number and zone. Only those properties within zones "A" and "V" require flood insurance. Zones "B" or "C" do not require flood insurance because FEMA designates only "A" and "V" zones as "Special Flood Hazard Areas."

120   The Uniform Residential Appraisal Report Handbook

IMPROVEMENTS:

GENERAL DESCRIPTION:

UNITS: Enter number of units being valued. The URAR is designed for 1-4 units.

STORIES: Enter the number of stories above grade not including the basement.

TYPE: Enter "Det." (detached), "S/D" (semi-detached) or "R" (Row).

DESIGN (STYLE): Enter brief description using local custom terminology. For example: Cape Cod, bi-level, split level, split foyer, townhouse, etc. Do not use builder's model name.

EXISTING: Enter "Yes" or "No."

PROPOSED: Enter "Yes" or "No."

UNDER CONSTRUCTION: Enter "Yes" or "No." A "Yes" requires plans and specs for the appraiser to review. If REHAB enter "REHAB" instead of "yes" or "no."

AGE (YRS.): Enter actual age. Construction records may be helpful if available.

EFFECTIVE AGE (YRS.): Enter effective age, if appropriate. This is judgmental. May want to report a range.

A difference between actual and effective age typically is caused by a level of maintenance or remodeling which may be below or above average. Significant differences between the actual and effective ages should be noted.

EXTERIOR DESCRIPTION:

FOUNDATION: Enter type of construction such as poured concrete, concrete block or wood.

EXTERIOR WALLS: Enter type of construction material such as aluminum, wood siding, brick veneer, porcelain, log, stucco. If combination show predominant portion first.

ROOF SURFACE: Enter type such as composition, wood, slate, tile.

GUTTERS & DOWNSPOUTS: Enter type such as galvanized, aluminum, wood, plastic. If partial, state location. If none, enter "None."

WINDOW TYPE: Describe type such as doublehung, casement, sliding. Identify the construction type such as aluminum, wood, or vinyl.

STORM SASH: Describe combination or style.

SCREENS: Enter "Yes" or "No." If partial, state location.

MANUFACTURED HOUSE: Enter either mobile home (MH) or modular (MOD.).

FOUNDATION:

SLAB	_____	Enter "Yes" or "No."
CRAWL SPACE	_____	Enter "Yes" or "No." If partial, include percentage of floor area.
BASEMENT	_____	Enter "Full," "Partial," or "None."
SUMP PUMP	_____	Enter "Yes" or "No."

DAMPNESS	_____	Enter "Yes" or "No."
SETTLEMENT	_____	Enter "Yes" or "No." Check for cracks.
INFESTATION	_____	Enter "Yes" or "None Apparent." Look for all types of insects and damage. If there is any question, require termite inspection.

BASEMENT:

AREA SQ. FT.	_____	Enter square feet.
% FINISHED	_____	Enter percentage of basement square footage (figure above) that is finished.
CEILING	_____	Enter material type.
WALLS	_____	Enter material type.
FLOOR	_____	Enter floor type. Comment if any part is dirt.
OUTSIDE ENTRY	_____	Enter "Yes" or "No." If "Yes," enter type.

INSULATION:

Roof _____ [ ]

Ceiling _____ [ ]

Walls _____ [ ]

Floor _____ [ ]

None _____ [ ]

Adequacy _____ [ ]

Make every effort to determine the type and R-Factor. If the existence of insulation cannot be determined, enter "unknown." Do not guess.

Enter in each blank line one of the following:
    G = Good
    A = Average
    F = Fair
    P = Poor
    U = Undetermined

Enter a [x] or [ ] in the box to denote the existence of insulation if the feature was verified. For example:
    "Walls __A__ [x]"
which means that wall insulation was verified and judged to be average

Energy Efficient Items:

Identify any special energy efficient items such as extra insulation, design of home, solar, earth sheltered, attic vents, heat pump.

ROOM LIST:

Questions concerning *room design* and *count* should reflect local custom.

Typically, a room totally underground is not as valuable as one above ground.

Typically, the foyer, bath, and laundry room are not counted as rooms. A room is a *livable area* with a *specific use*.

A dining area built as an L-shape off the kitchen may or may not be a room depending upon the size. A simple test which may be used to determine whether one or two rooms should be counted is to hypothetically insert a wall to separate the two areas which have been built as one. If the residents can utilize the resulting two rooms with the same or more utility and without increased inconvenience, the room count should be two. If the existence of the hypothetical wall would result in a lack of utility and increased inconvenience, the room count should be one.

The room count typically includes a living room (LR), dining room (DR), kitchen (KT), Den (DN), recreation room (REC), and bedroom (BR).

The following definitions and terms may be useful as a guide:

Basement:	Generally *completely below* the grade. This is *NOT* counted in the finished gross living area at the grade level.
Level 1:	Includes all finished living area at the grade level.
Level 2:	Includes all finished area above the first level.
Foyer:	Entrance hall of a house.

In completing this section, enter the *number* of each room type on each level. *DO NOT* enter the dimensions.

Area Sq. Ft.: Calculate the overall square footage of each level from the exterior dimensions.

    Square Feet of Gross Living Area: Enter total square footage *above grade*.

INTERIOR:

SURFACES	Materials/ Conditions	Make every effort to describe accurately.
Floors	_____	Enter type such as tile, hardwood or carpet.
Walls	_____	Enter type such as plaster, drywall or paneled.
Trim/Finish	_____	Enter type of moldings such as wood, metal or vinyl.
Bath Floor	_____	Enter ceramic, vinyl tile, or carpet.
Bath Wainscot	_____	Enter type that protects walls from moisture, such as ceramic tile or fiberglass.
Doors	_____	Enter wood or steel.
_____		
_____		
Fireplace(s) _____	_____	Enter type such as brick or steel free-standing. Enter the number of fireplaces.

HEATING

Type	_____	Enter type: hot water, steam, forced warm air, gravity warm air, radiant.
Fuel	_____	Enter fuel: coal, gas, oil, electric, wood.
Condition	_____	Enter condition: "Good," "Average," "Fair," or "Poor." Be sure to explain "Fair" or "Poor" rating.
Adequacy	_____	Describe adequacy: Does system heat the house well? Use "Good," "Average," "Fair," or "Poor." Explain a "Fair" or "Poor" rating.

COOLING:

Central	_____	Enter "Yes" or "No."
Other	_____	Describe.
Condition	_____	Describe as with Heating.
Adequacy	_____	Describe as with Heating.

KITCHEN EQUIPMENT: Make an entry in the boxes to indicate that these items exist. An entry in a box means that these items were seen and they are fixtures. An item that was seen but is personal property should have a "P" in the box and not be included in value.

ATTIC: Additional space such as an attic or room above the garage should be described in the manner in which it can be actually used. The essential question is whether it can be included in the above-grade living area.

IMPROVEMENT ANALYSIS:

QUALITY OF CONSTRUCTION: Look for quality and durability.

CONDITION OF IMPROVEMENTS: Look for physical deterioration. If the value is subject to completion of repairs and alterations, rate the property after completion. An example could be a property which is observed to be 'fair' but the appraisal is subject to repairs being completed which could warrant a "good" rating. The rating "good" is then appropriate. Also, an appraisal on property being constructed would be rated as though finished.

ROOM SIZES/LAYOUT: While a property might be "average" it still may suffer from functional obsolescence. The particular feature in question may exist in all of the comparables selected, in which case all would be classified as "average."

ENERGY EFFICIENT: Relative to local standards.

PLUMBING - ADEQUACY & CONDITION: Look for style and condition of fixtures. Include comments concerning condition of septic system if applicable.

ELECTRICAL - ADEQUACY & CONDITION: Relative to local staandards. G-A-F-P.

ESTIMATED REMAINING ECONOMIC LIFE: Enter the number of years the property is expected to remain competitive in the market. You should use 40 years unless an obvious and verifiable pressure exists which can be conclusively shown to render the remaining economic life to be less than 40 years.

ESTIMATED REMAINING PHYSICAL LIFE: To be used only in cases where the property is located in a 223(e) area in which the economic life is waived and physical life is used instead.

COMMENTS:

ADDITIONAL FEATURES: Enter here any additional features such as a pool, special fireplace features or other features not shown above or any comments you may wish to make.

DEPRECIATION COMMENTS: Enter repairs needed, modernization, etc.

GENERAL MARKET CONDITIONS: Financing concessions for the subject and the market area should be explained. Be sure to explain whether the subject is consistent with the market area or different.

BACK PAGE OF URAR FORM

BUILDING SKETCH (SHOW GROSS LIVING AREA ABOVE GRADE): Sketch should include all exterior dimensions of house as well as patios, porches, garages, breezeways and other offsets. State "covered" or "uncovered" to indicate a roof or no roof such as over a patio.

COST APPROACH: The estimated reproduction cost, new, of improvements, need not be completed; however, the estimated value of the *site* must be entered. If the subject property is proposed construction or existing construction under one year of age, the Marshall and Swift Form 1007 is to be completed and attached, in conformance with Deputy Assistant Secretary Nistler's Memorandum of Instructions dated December 17, 1985.

DOES PROPERTY CONFORM TO APPLICABLE MINIMUM HUD/VA STANDARDS?

This question refers not only to standards as set forth in HUD Handbook 4905.1, but also to hazards of lead based paint. If the property was built prior to 1973 and there is no evidence of cracking, chipping, peeling or loose paint, then, insofar as the lead based paint issue is concerned, the question may be answered "yes." However, if such a deficiency exists, the question must be answered "no" and under explanation state "property built prior to 1973. Lead based paint abatement required." In addition, the appraiser must check the lead based paint abatement requirement on the V.C. sheet.

CONSTRUCTION WARRANTY: Determine if property will be covered by a construction warranty such as H.O.W., H.B.W. or other HUD-approved warranty and enter information. Check "Yes" box only if warranty plan is HUD-approved.

SALES COMPARISON ANALYSIS: *All adjustments must be extracted from the market.*

ADDRESS: Enter address that can be used to locate each property. Enter community, if needed to identify property. For rural properties, list location by road name, nearest intersection, and side of road.

PROXIMITY TO SUBJECT: Enter proximity "as the crow flies." Enter description like "3 houses W subject." If comparable is more than 1 mile from subject, be sure to explain in the "Comments" section.

SALES PRICE: Enter total paid by buyer, including extras.

PRICE/GROSS LIV. AREA: Enter price per square foot for living area above grade.

DATA SOURCE: Enter source name, or others such as tax stamps, MLS, etc. This is the data source for the price and property information. Also show type of financing such as Conv., FHA or VA.

SALES OR FINANCING CONCESSIONS: Enter adjustment for sales concessions, if needed. Be sure to explain in "Comments" section and use Addendum if appropriate.

The adjustment for sales or financing concessions is done here, if applicable. Each comparable is adjusted in accordance with instructions contained in Mortgagee Letter 86-15.

Always select the comparables with the fewest dissimilarities. Use older sales only if more recent ones are not available and be sure to explain their use in the "Comments" section.

The value factors of Location, Site/View, Design and Appeal, Quality of Construction, Age, Condition, and Functional Utility are all subjective factors that require subjective adjustments. Be careful that your adjustments are reasonable—not excessive. If a property is ever overvalued, a high probability exists that the reason can be traced to an excessive adjustment somewhere in this section.

DATE OF SALE/TIME: Enter month and year. This date refers to a date of closing. A specific day is not necessary unless it is meaningful, such as in a rapidly changing market.

LOCATION: Enter "Good," "Average," or "Fair," when compared to the subject and using the same standard as the subject.

SITE/VIEW: Enter size of lot and explain view if appropriate. Adjustments come from a view which has been rated as "superior" or "inferior" to the subject as well as size of lot. Small differences in lot sizes do not usually call for an adjustment if the size is typical.

DESIGN AND APPEAL: Enter the style according to a description used by local custom and show appeal as G-A-F-P.

QUALITY OF CONSTRUCTION: Enter "Good," "Average," or "Fair" and the construction type such as aluminum siding, wood siding, brick, etc.

AGE: If both actual and effective age are used, enter both such as "A-25, E-20." A difference typically is caused by modernization or significant maintenance, or the lack of either. A difference is the basis for a (+) or (−) adjustment.

CONDITION: Enter "Good," "Average," "Fair," or "Poor" when compared to the subject. Be consistent with Side 1.

ABOVE GRADE ROOM COUNT GROSS LIVING AREA: Enter room count, which should be consistent with Side 1. Commonly, three adjustments may be entered. For example, the first may be an adjustment for "expendable space" such as a bath. A deficiency in the number of baths should be adjusted first. The second is a separate adjustment for a difference in square feet. The third is an adjustment for room count. These can be individual or separate adjustments which have been combined. All should be extracted from the market.

Typically, an appraiser will *not* make an adjustment for square feet difference *and* a difference in the room count. An example where it could occur is a very large home with a small room count. Any property that has an adjustment in square feet and room count should be explained.

BASEMENT & FINISHED ROOMS BELOW GRADE: Enter the type of improvements in the basement such as bedroom, rec room, laundry, etc. Explain any special features. Show number of square feet of *finished* area.

FUNCTIONAL UTILITY: Enter "equal," "superior," or "inferior," as a total of the items rated in the Improvement Analysis compared to the subject. Be consistent with the factors reported there. Use "Comments" section frequently and explain special features.

The category of functional utility typically is the place to deduct for functional obsolescence which has been observed in the subject and recorded on Side 1 and which is not found in the comparables. Dollar adjustments should be extracted from the market. For example, a poor floor design that includes two bedrooms which are located so that entrance to one is gained by passing through the other typically requires a negative adjustment for functional obsolescence. In such a case, the second bedroom would not be counted as a bedroom.

HEATING/COOLING: Enter an adjustment for heating and cooling systems, if appropriate. Any adjustments should be based upon local market expectations.

GARAGE/CARPORT: Enter an adjustment for car storage. Adjustments should be calculated in accordance with market acceptance of carport value versus garage and size.

PORCHES, PATIO, POOLS, ETC.: Enter an adjustment for these features. Any adjustments should be based upon local market expectations. For example, a pool located in an area that expects pools might bring a dollar premium in comparison to a comparable without a pool. However, a pool located in a low-income area might bring a negative adjustment resulting from an increase in maintenance.

SPECIAL ENERGY EFFICIENT ITEMS: Enter an adjustment for any energy efficient items such as storm windows and doors, solar installations, etc.

FIREPLACE(S): Enter any adjustment for the presence (or absence) of fireplace.

OTHER (E.G., KITCHEN EQUIPMENT, REMODELING): Enter adjustments for any features not covered elsewhere.

NET. ADJ. (TOTAL): Check either [+] or [−] box to indicate if the total net adjustments will increase or decrease the sales price. If any adjustment is excessive, the comparables should be reviewed to determine if the best ones were selected. Any adjustment which appears to be excessive should be explained.

INDICATED VALUE OF SUBJECT: The appraiser needs to watch the magnitude of the adjustments by comparing each one to the sales price. Generally, the total adjustments should not exceed 10% of the sale price.

Total all of the adjustments and add or subtract them to the sales price of each comparable.

INCOME APPROACH: The Income Approach need be completed only for three and four-unit properties. When used, the appraiser is to show the gross rent from each of the comparables at the bottom of the form under "Final Reconciliation" as: Comp. #1 Gross Rent = $1,000.00; Comp. #2 Gross Rent = $1,200.00 ...", etc.

If the Income Approach is not used, the appraiser should draw a line through the words "Indicated Value by Income Approach (if applicable)" and enter the estimated market rent. The rest of the line items should be marked "N/A."

Check the box marked "as is" or "subject to repairs ...".

COMMENTS AND CONDITIONS OF APPRAISAL: In addition to any comments which the appraiser wishes to make, the appraiser should enter the monthly expenses estimated for: maintenance and repairs, heat and utilities, real estate taxes, fire insurance closing costs and condominium or PUD common expense as appropriate. The appraiser must also enter VC requirements codes, such as "VC 21, 28 and 30."

FINAL RECONCILIATION: This entry should contain the appraiser's reasoning for arriving at the final value. The appraiser must sign his/her name, print name under signature with assigned CHUMS identification number and date report as of the day inspected. The Reviewer also signs, dates and writes CHUMS identification number at the bottom of the report as of date of review and then completes the Data Entry Sheet.

VA GUIDELINES

January 16, 1987   DVB CIRCULAR 26-87-5
EXHIBIT B

TO: All Fee Appraisers

SUBJ: Uniform Residential Appraisal Report

   a. *Subject Section*, "Property Rights Appraised" - Since VA will utilize this form for all PUD (planned-unit development) types, the word "De Minimis" should be deleted in all instances. The required reporting of assessment fees (condominium or PUD) shall be made in the "Comments" block of the Site section.

   b. *Subject Section*, "Loan charges/concessions to be paid by seller $" - The appraiser is not required to investigate and complete this block. However, if the information is known, it should be provided.

   c. *Site Section*, "FEMA Flood Hazard" - If the appraiser indicates that the property is located in a special flood hazard area, as identified by FEMA (Federal Emergency Management Agency), the map number and designated zone must be provided.

   d. *Improvements Section*, "Exterior Description" - In addition to noting their composition, appraisers will indicate the observed condition of the foundation, exterior walls, roof surface, gutters and downspouts, and windows by using the following notations: "G" (good), "A" (average), "F" (fair) or "P" (poor).

   NOTE: When "P" (poor) is noted as the condition of *any* item on the URAR, the appraiser must indicate in the Comments section, or on an attached sheet, the required MPR (Minimum Property Requirement) repairs or provide a statement explaining why repairs are not recommended.

   e. *Sales Comparison Analysis Section* - Appraisers need not compute the "Price/Gross Living Area" for the subject property or the comparables unless it is considered a valid method of comparison.

   f. *Sales Comparison Analysis Section* - The appraiser *must* consider and report the effect of any sales or financing incentives involved in the comparable sales transactions. The appraiser must provide an adequate, supportable explanation of any adjustments made to the comparables. That explanation shall appear in the "Comments On Sales Comparison" block or by attachment. Fee appraisers are directed to local release #_____ (DVB Circular 26-86-9, par. 4f) which states VA's policy regarding seller incentives. In the Comments section, under "General market conditions and prevalence and impact in subject/market area regarding loan discounts, interest buydowns and concessions", fee appraisers *must* in each and every case, proposed or existing, report the *existence or nonexistence* of sales or financing incentives or concessions in the subject market area and make a statement regarding their effect, if any, on the sales prices of comparable homes. The appraiser is not required to investigate incentives or concessions involving the subject property. Statements made here must be consistent with the "Sales Comparison Analysis".

   • In addition to those areas discussed in paragraph 6, certain portions of the URAR are not required to be completed by the fee appraiser (unless a regional office requirement) for VA loan guaranty purposes. Those portions are:

a. *Subject Section* - "Lender Discretionary Use" is completed by the lender at their discretion.

b. *Cost Approach Section* - "Building Sketch" is not required to be completed unless the appraiser needs to illustrate unique features of the subject or presence of functional obsolescence, etc.

c. *Cost Approach Section* - only the "Estimated Site Value" must be completed in every case proposed or existing (condominiums excluded).

d. *Indicated Value by Income Approach Section* - This section will be completed only if applicable and a valid indicator of value (e.g., multi-unit building).

• Fee appraisers will continue to provide the regional office with an additional copy of each appraisal report. The requirement for photographs remains unchanged.

• VA Form 26-1805, Request for Determination of Reasonable Value, is being revised. The revised VA Form 26-1805 package will not contain the appraisal report form (URAR). As previously stated, the URAR will be obtained from private sources. Instructions concerning the revised VA Form 26-1805 package will be issued separately. Fee appraisers who complete the URAR during the transition period (until April 30, 1987) may retain the unused VA forms 26-1803 for use as they see fit.

• As we have indicated, certain portions of the URAR are not required to be completed by the fee appraiser for VA loan guaranty purposes. In concept, however, the appraisal report's commonality should allow it to be used for other than VA loan guaranty purposes (e.g., an appraisal completed on this form could be used for conventional loan purposes should the veteran not qualify for a VA-assisted loan). In such cases the requester may require that the fee appraiser complete the appraisal form in its entirety. Requesters who wish to have the entire appraisal form completed will make arrangements directly with the fee appraiser. In those cases in which the appraiser is requested to complete the form in its entirety, any additional expense involved cannot be charged to the veteran. The additional expense must be born by some other party (i.e., the seller or mortgage).

• Fee appraisers are reminded that their role is to provide the VA with an adequately supported estimate of market value of an accurately described subject property. Fee appraisers are required to render a value estimate in accordance with the Veterans Administration's regulatory definition of reasonable value (38 CFR 36.4301). The regulatory definition of reasonable value is "that figure which represents the amount a reputable and qualified appraiser, unaffected by personal interest, bias, or prejudice, would recommend to a prospective purchaser as a proper price or cost in the light of prevailing conditions". The VA considers reasonable value and market value to be synonymous. The VA definition of market value is considered consistent with that used by Fannie Mae, Freddie Mac and the two major appraisal organizations. That definition directs appraisers to determine "the most probable price which a property should bring, or for which the appraised property should sell, in a competitive market, under all conditions requisite to a fair sale, with the buyer and seller each acting prudently, knowledgeably, and assuming the price is not affected by undue stimulus".

• It is the VA fee appraiser's responsibility to develop a market value for the subject property which is consistent with the current standard definition of market value and the VA regulatory definition of reasonable value.

FARMERS HOME ADMINISTRATION GUIDELINES

FORM FmHA 1922-8

Used to prepare written appraisal reports on single family residences on non-farm tracts, small farms and leasehold interest for FmHA loanmaking, inventory sales and servicing purposes.

Adequate narrative documentation may be made on reverse or attachments as necessary to document legal descriptions, etc., and support value estimates. Calculations used in the cost approach (Form 1007, "Square Foot Appraisal Form") will always be attached. At least one photograph of existing dwellings will be attached.

INSTRUCTIONS FOR PREPARATION

This form was developed for use by FmHA, VA, HUD, Freddie Mac and Fannie Mae and contains some items that reflect identical information reported on Form 1007, "Square Foot Appraisal Form", and are not required to be repeated on Form 1922-8 for FmHA appraisals. If space on Form FmHA 1922-8 is not adequate to record the information required herein, an addendum may be attached or the information recorded on the reverse of the form.

1. Enter FmHA case number.
2. Enter address that can be used to locate the property. Do not use Post Office box numbers. If necessary, attach direction map to appraisal report. Complete all information requested and attach a copy of the legal description to the property, which provides a full and proper legal description, including restrictions, easements and reservations, as appropriate.
3. For loan making purposes, enter loan applicants name. For servicing purposes, enter borrowers or advice number.
4. Check appropriate box.
5. Leave Blank.
6. Check appropriate box.
7. Check appropriate box.
8. Enter percentage of predominant use within the neighborhood. All figures should total 100 percent.
9. Enter potential for change in use within the neighborhood, within the next 3 to 5 years.
10. Enter predominant occupancy in neighborhood, "Vacant" refers to finished buildings. If vacancy exceeds 10 percent, provide comments on the absorption potential, supply, and demand factors.
11. Enter the predominant Low and High prices within the neighborhood, after excluding the extremes.

12. Summarize Neighborhood Analysis comments in this section. All items in the Neighborhood Analysis section rated "Fair/Poor" must be explained.

13. Enter site dimensions. If irregular, enter total square footage; or if more than one acre, enter the number of acres in "site area". Complete All Questions.

14. Indicate conditions observed. FEMA is the Federal Emergency Management Agency.

15. Identify utilities available for use to the site.

16. Indicate site improvements.

17. Enter comments as appropriate to the site.

18. Leave Blank. Complete on Form 1007.

19. Leave Blank. Complete on Form 1007.

20. Leave Blank. Complete on Form 1007.

21. Leave Blank. Complete on Form 1007.

22. Indicate R-Factor on insulation. If the existence of insulation on Existing homes cannot be determined, enter "unknown".

23. Indicate the number of rooms and the gross square feet of living area as defined in FmHA Instruction 1944-A, §1944.16. Basement areas completely below grade, are not considered in the finished gross living area above grade.

    The total gross living area will be used to determine eligibility for FmHA Rural Housing Program Assistance.

24. Indicate appropriate type and condition for existing homes only.

25. Indicate appropriate type and condition.

26. Check appropriate box.

27. Check appropriate box.

28. Indicate conditions.

29. Leave Blank. Complete on Form 1007.

30. Describe additional improvements or comment on conditions.

30a. Describe any observed physical, functional or external inadequacies which decrease value. All types of Obsolescence are reported in this section.

30b. Indicate financing concessions for the subject property and market area.

31. Leave Blank. Complete on Form 1007 (reverse side). ATTACH RECENT PHOTOGRAPH OF EXISTING HOME IN THIS SECTION.

32. Complete the "Indicated Value by Cost Approach". ($ value) is defined from Form 1007, line 34.

33. Note building code standard(s) used.

34. Leave Blank.
35. Leave Blank.
36. Enter address, sufficiently complete, that can be used to identify and locate the comparable sale; such as house and street numbers.
37. Enter proximity of comparable to subject. If comparable property is more than one mile from subject, explain in "Comments" section.
38. Enter confirmed sales price for comparables.
39. Leave Blank.
40. Enter source name.
41. Describe sale concessions. Provide additional comments in the "Comments" section or use Addendum if needed.
41a. All adjustments of the comparable property to the subject property will be indicated by a (+ or −) dollar value; Comparable Better (CBS); Subject Better (SBA). SUPPORT ALL ADJUSTMENTS. Use Addendum if necessary.
42. Indicate Month and Year of each comparable.
42a. Enter appropriate adjustment.
43. Indicate Good, Average or Fair.
43a. Enter appropriate adjustment.
44. Indicate either Superior, Average or Inferior.
44a. Enter appropriate adjustment.
45. Indicate building design.

Type of design:	Abbreviation:
Cape Cod	CC
Bi-Level	Bi-L
Split Foyer	SpF
Two Story	2ST
Ranch	Ran
Manufactured	Mft

This section applies to the desirability of the exterior and interior features of the dwelling. Avoid using comparable properties which are dissimilar to the subject e.g., Two Story comparable versus a Ranch style subject property.

REMEMBER, COMPARE APPLES versus APPLES!!

45a. Enter appropriate adjustment.
46. Indicate Marshall-Swift Classification.
46a. Enter appropriate adjustment.

47. Indicate Effective Age and/or Actual Age (please specify).

   Example: Effective age is 10 years and in good condition = E-10/G.

   This criteria will be used for the Subject and Comparables.

47a. Enter appropriate adjustment.

48. Indicate "Good", "Average", "Fair", or "Poor".

48a. Enter appropriate adjustment.

49. Overall Room Count and corresponding gross living area for FmHA purposes, is defined in FmHA Instruction 1944-A, § 1944.16.

49a. Enter appropriate information.

50. Basement and Basement Finished rooms below grade.

   Indicate total area in basement and area of finished in basement.

50a. Enter appropriate adjustment.

51. Enter "Superior", "Equal", or "Inferior", as a total of the items rated in the Improvements Analysis section of the appraisal.

51a. Enter appropriate adjustment.

52. Complete as appropriate.

52a. Enter adjustment for heating and cooling systems.

53. Complete as appropriate.

53a. Enter adjustment for Garage/Carport and or outside storage areas. (Include attached or detached).

54. Complete as appropriate.

54a. Enter adjustment for these features.

55. Complete as appropriate.

55a. FmHA Thermal Standards can be adjusted in this section.

56. Complete as appropriate.

56a. All adjustments should be market extracted.

57. Complete as appropriate.

57a. Enter adjustments for features not covered elsewhere in the appraisal report, e.g., Common elements and assessments, kitchen equipment.

58. Net adjustments normally should not exceed 15 percent of the sales price. Gross adjustments normally should not exceed 25 percent of the sales price.

59. Indicate value of subject. Subtract net adjustments from the sales price.

134   The Uniform Residential Appraisal Report Handbook

60. Enter comments on sales comparison. Use Addendum if necessary to support all adjustments in this section.

61. Complete after analyzing indicated values, in line 59.

62. Leave Blank. Complete for Non-Program Inventory Appraisals only.

63. Leave Blank. Complete for Non-Program Inventory Appraisals only.

64. Leave Blank. Complete for Non-Program Inventory Appraisals only.

65. Indicate appropriate block upon which the appraisal was made and provide additional comments.

66. Enter a brief statement concerning the basis of the final reconciliation, including the type and availability of the data.

67. Check appropriate box.

68. Enter date property was inspected by the appraiser and the market value of the subject property which is based upon analysis of the market data and cost approach, in accordance with FmHA Instruction 1922-C.

69. Signature of appraiser.

70. Signature of review appraiser, as appropriate.

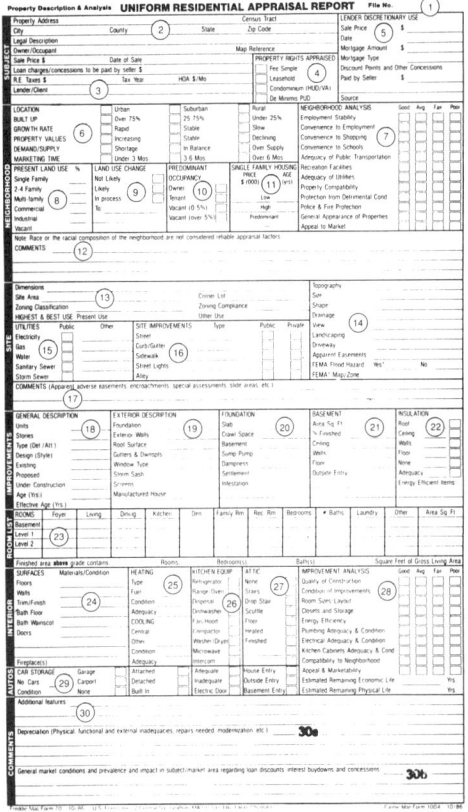
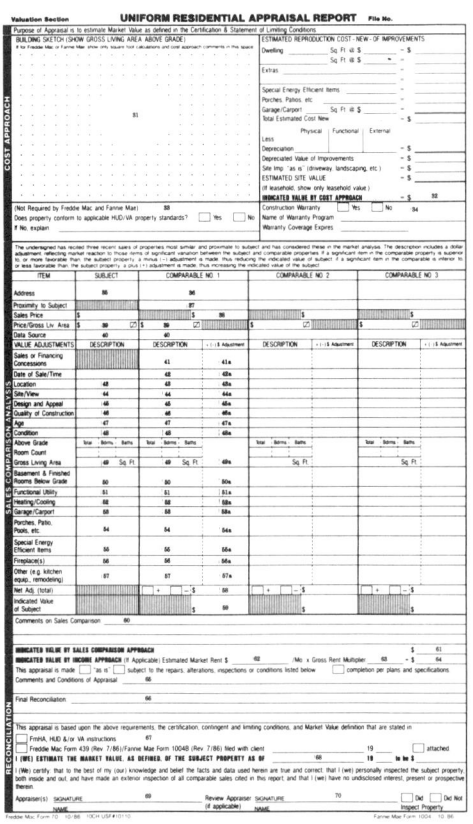

Reviewing Guidelines

for the

Uniform Residential Appraisal Report

SUBJECT SECTION

1. The appraiser should complete the subject section of the report utilizing information supplied by the client as well as from data contained in the appraiser's own reference materials. Information should be verified by reviewing tax bills, plats of survey and other recognized real estate records and source books.

2. Check census tract, map references and zip code numbers. These items are frequently left out of the report. Missing information in any section of the report is a sign that the appraiser has not handled the appraisal assignment in a thorough and thoughtful manner.

3. It is the appraiser's responsibility to complete the Form in its entirety except for the box titled "Lender Discretionary Use." The purpose of this box is to encourage lenders to provide closing dates to comparable sales reporting services. If the lender completes this section, it should do so after the loan settlement.

4. If the appraiser has checked the box De Minimus PUD, the appraiser must provide the monthly homeowner's association fee for de minimus PUD units. In addition, the appraiser must describe the project amenities in the "Neighborhood" section and address their effect on marketability and value.

NEIGHBORHOOD SECTION

5. The neighborhood section of the appraisal report should be complete and accurate. Location is a critical factor with respect to a property's value and marketability. Information in this section is also vitally important as financial institutions must evaluate loan packages based upon their underwriting standards. Complete and accurate information is necessary in order to make sound underwriting decisions. What a company doesn't know *can* hurt it!

6. Factors in the neighborhood section must be carefully handled by the appraiser. Since financial institutions are concerned with risk, underwriters working for these organizations are attempting to visualize both the neighborhood and surrounding market in order to spot healthy growth patterns versus undesirable trends that may indicate a deteriorating neighborhood with limited market appeal. For example, a property located in an over built area where values are steeply declining and marketing time is lengthy may be an unacceptable risk to a financial institution.

7. Comments in the neighborhood section must be relevant and give insight into those factors which positively or negatively affect the appraised property's marketability. A neighborhood should be acceptable to a large enough segment of buyers to support an active market. In brief, a property should have potential for long-term acceptance and be relatively free of detrimental conditions.

8. All fair and poor ratings in the neighborhood analysis section must be explained. Negative factors may adversely affect the value and long-term marketability of a property. The ratings on the appraisal form have been specially selected to represent items that are important to buyers in the market place. Low rating need to be addressed since financial institutions are concerned with market strength over a long period of time.

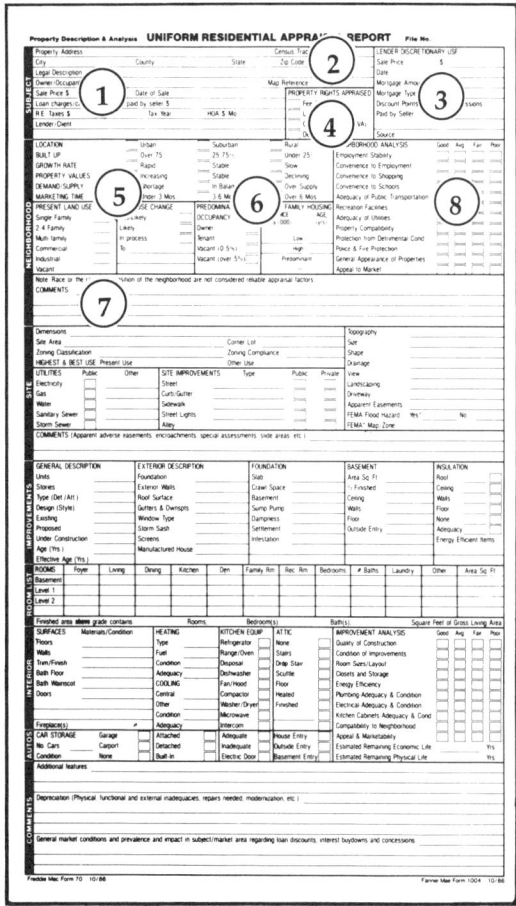

NEIGHBORHOOD SECTION (cont'd.)

9 The appraiser should comment when the neighborhood is experiencing a decline in values. Due to a loss in equity, a property located in a neighborhood or area where values are declining may present a financial institution with a high and perhaps unacceptable risk. Financial organizations expect that loan amortization will keep up with or exceed any decline in prices. Therefore, stable or rising property values with average or above ratings for the improvements are important considerations in underwriting any given loan.

10 Residential properties that are near the top or above the top of the neighborhood value range may present a high risk to financial institutions. The appraiser should comment on properties that are valued at 90% or more of the highest property value in the neighborhood. Such properties may represent over improvements and be difficult to sell in a reasonable length of time. The appraiser's comments can clarify whether or not a property lacks marketability because it represents an over improvement for the area.

11 When there is an over supply of housing this factor must be addressed by the appraiser. An over supply of housing is a critical factor as it may result in limited marketability and produce a decline in values. Financial institutions in underwriting loans in overbuilt markets can experience substantial losses. Frequently, appraisal reports fail to inform financial institutions of declining values and marketability problems. Financial organizations wish to obtain insight into the reasons for market rejection in a given geographic area or neighborhood.

12 The appraiser should comment when marketing time is over six months. A lengthy marketing time poses special problems as it reflects a slow market and usually declining values. In a slow or declining market, the borrowers may be placed in a position where it is impossible for them to dispose of their property. An erosion in values can result in a substantial loss for the financial institution.

SITE SECTION

13 Unfavorable site factors must be commented on by the appraiser. Financial institutions wish to know that site features such as size, shape and topography, etc. are acceptable in the market place. In brief, a site should meet all the criteria for a desirable lot in the area. A poor lot may result in poor marketability for the subject property.

14 The appraisal report should explain the affect on marketability of any unfavorable site conditions such as adverse easements, encroachments or other detrimental factors.

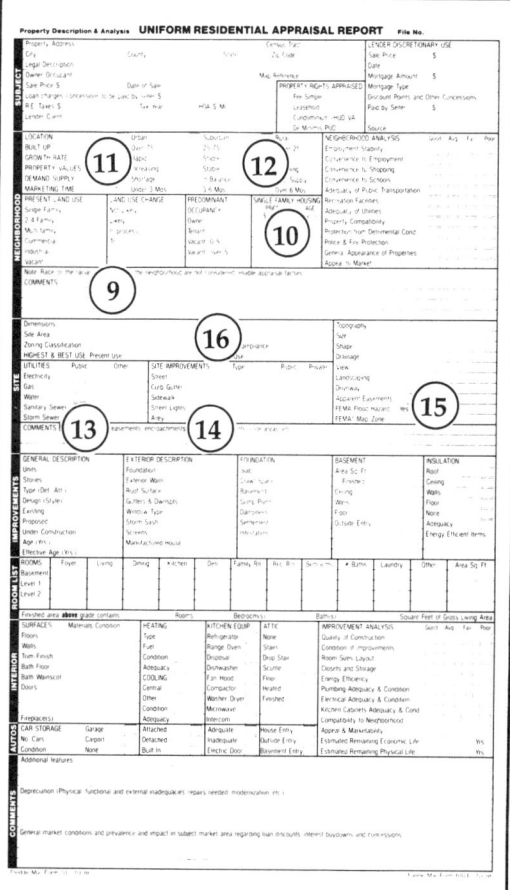

15 Problems relating to poor drainage and/or flood conditions must be dealt with by the appraiser in the comment section or attachments. If the appraiser indicates that the property is located in a Special Flood Hazard Area – as identified by the Federal Emergency Management Agency (FEMA) – the map number and designated zone must be noted. A financial institution may need to seek additional information to determine if the degree of risk is acceptable.

16 The appraiser should verify zoning for the subject and surrounding properties and give careful consideration to the appraisal property's highest and best use. If the improvements do not represent a legal, conforming use under the current zoning classification, the appraiser must clarify whether the subject's use is "legal non-conforming" or "illegal." The underwriter may wish to clarify non-compliance with zoning regulations, as non-compliance may have a significant impact on value and marketability.

IMPROVEMENT SECTION (etc.)

17 The appraiser must comment on functional and physical inadequacies and indicate when repairs or modernization are needed. Serious attention must be given to structural problems.

18 Fair or poor ratings for improvements must be explained. Such factors may adversely affect the property's long-term marketability. They may also limit the buyer's commitment to the property and loan.

19 Over and under-improvements deserve special comments. An over-improvements represents a higher risk than typical properties in the neighborhood. Further, their construction cost may be greater than their market value. Since cost and value can be quite different, the appraiser's value conclusion should reflect and be consistent with market information. When appraising recently built custom homes, the appraiser should be careful not to confuse the concept of cost with the concept of value.

20 The appraiser should comment on unusual layouts, peculiar floor plans, inadequate equipment and amenities. These factors limit value and market appeal and are important to the underwriter in determining the property's suitability for long-term high ratio financing.

21 If the appraiser is using computer generated data, facts and comments on the report must be applicable to the subject and comparable properties. Each property is unique. Therefore, comments and factual data will vary depending on the nature of the property. The appraiser should avoid using the computer to produce cookie-cutter appraisal reports. A computer is a tool to aid the appraiser. It is not to be used as a substitute for thinking.

22 If there is evidence of dampness, termites or settlement, the appraiser must comment on these factors as such conditions require careful documentation. In brief, the financial institution's underwriters will have to determine the severity of the condition, etc.

ANALYSIS SECTION

23 In estimating the cost approach, the appraiser should show measurements and state the subject's total gross living area. If the form does not provide sufficient space, the gross living area calculations can be shown on the floor plan sketch either within the cost approach section or in the exhibit section of the report.

24 In estimating reproduction costs, the appraiser should use cost figures that are appropriate for the local market. Further, the appraiser should attempt to be as accurate as possible with land costs as the value of land in proportion to the value of the total property is an important underwriting consideration.

25 An appraiser should not enter cost data into the market approach to value. For example, adjustments for gross living area should reflect what buyers are paying in the market place for specific value elements. Such adjustments should not represent preselected cost data which is applied equally to all types of living space.

26 All comparables must be recently closed sales of similar properties from the subject neighborhood. Good appraisal reports all have one thing in common: the appraiser has selected good comparable data which has been well handled.

27 The appraiser must avoid using old comparables. Sales should have occurred within the last three months. Any sales that are over three months old must be explained. Markets change, and sometimes swiftly. Therefore, it is important that appraisers use the most recent sales available.

28 Comparables must be similar in design and style. They should contain, if possible, the same room count and approximate square foot area. Dissimilar properties should not be used as comparables.

29 All sales should be transactions that have closed. The appraiser should not adjust contracts or listings. A meeting of the minds in a real estate transaction involves something more than a sales contract. It involves the ability to go to the closing table and complete the transaction. Recorded data can be adequately verified and has a much higher degree of validity than word of mouth information from brokers and builders. Contracts frequently do not make it to closing. When they do, details of the transactions sometimes change before closing. In brief, contracts may not reflect a property's market value.

30 If the appraiser has obtained contract or listing data which the appraiser feels deserves consideration, this information can be placed in the comment or addenda section of the report.

31 Except for rural locations, all sales must be from the neighborhood. A range of one mile will usually encompass the neighborhood for most properties. The appraiser should be familiar with the neighborhood boundaries. However, it is always good practice to find properties as close to the subject as possible.

32 Appraisers must not engage in excessive adjusting. Large adjustments indicate that the comps are not comparable. Large upward adjustments can be a clue that the appraiser is pumping value. Total gross adjustments on all comparables must not exceed 25% of the sales price. Individual line adjustments must not be greater than 10% of the sales price. In brief, the appraiser's adjustments should be realistic.

ANALYSIS SECTION (cont'd.)

33 The appraiser should attempt to bracket the sales data before making adjustments. In brief, find properties that are a little better than the subject and those that are not quite as good, as well as a range in between. This will enable the appraiser to establish a tight value range. Proper bracketing aids the appraiser in producing a convincing appraisal report.

34 Time adjustments must reflect the market. The appraiser should avoid making upward adjustment in a flat or declining market. This can result in a property being substantially over appraised.

35 Personal property must not be included in the market value of the subject. Chattel property is not eligible for mortgage financing.

36 Sales and financing concessions must be properly handled by the appraiser. The value of giveaway items such as cars and boats must also be explained in the appraisal report. The area for the sales for financing concession data for the subject property is shaded in the sales comparison analysis adjustment grid. The appraiser must state the specific information for the property in the "subject" section or in the "comments" section on the first page. Also, the appraiser must include the specific sales or financing concession information for the comparable sales – such as the mortgage amount, interest rate, loan type, and any loan fees or concessions that the seller paid.

For special or creative financing or for sales concessions, the comparable sales must be adjusted to the market at the time of the comparable sales, not to the subject property. No adjustments are necessary for those costs that are normally paid by sellers because of tradition or law in a market area – these costs are readily identifiable since the seller pays them in virtually all sales transactions. Special or creative financing adjustments can be made to a comparable property by comparing the financing terms offered by a third party institutional lender that is not involved in the property or transaction. Any adjustment should not be calculated on a mechanical dollar-for-dollar cost for the financing or concession – the dollar amount of any adjustment should approximate the market's reaction to the financing or concessions based on the appraiser's judgment.

37 The appraiser will check the appropriate boxes and complete the comments and reconciliation sections under the sales comparison grid. The appraisal must be based on the definition of market value, that is stated in the Certification and Statement of Limiting Conditions. If the Freddie Mac Form 439 (Rev. 7/86) and Fannie Mae Form 1004B (Rev. 7/86) has not been filed with the Lender, it should be attached to the Appraisal Report currently being submitted.

38 If the appraiser has selected good comparable market data and handled it well, the adjusted sales should fall into a tight range. The final conclusion of value should relate to the adjusted comparables. It is appropriate for the appraiser to base a value conclusion on the adjusted value of the best comparable.

39 The appraiser will type his or her name under the signature line.

THE AUTHORITATIVE SOURCE

The Appraisal Review & Mortgage Underwriting Journal

For Intriguing Articles on Today's Current Issues of Interest To The Reviewer & Mortgage Underwriter

 It is the only authoritative source available on the specialized areas of Appraisal Review & Mortgage Underwriting.

 The information is presented in a practical, how to do style and is written by individuals who are active in the profession.

 The subject matter is current and designed to keep readers abreast of the current trends and changes affecting the Appraisal Review & Mortgage Underwriting Industry.

Don't Miss This Educational Offering! Subscribe Today and Learn How to Review & Underwrite More Effectively!

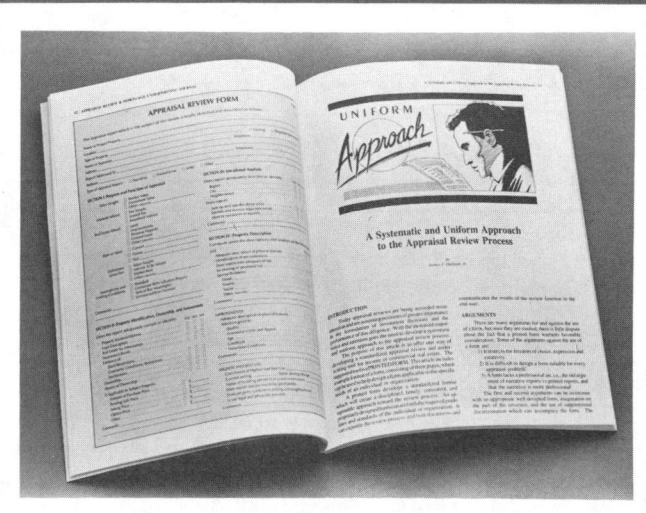

National Association of Review Appraisers & Mortgage Underwriters
8715 Via De Commercio • Scottsdale, Arizona 85258
(602) 998-3000

☐ **YES** I want to keep abreast of the current trends and changes affecting the Appraisal Review & Mortgage Underwriting Industry. Enclosed is my check for $32.00 for 1 year's subscription (3 issues). I understand if at any time I am not completely satisfied with my subscription to the Appraisal Review & Mortgage Underwriting Journal, I may cancel and receive a refund for my unexpired subscription.

Name _____ Title _____
Business Affiliation _____
Address _____
City _____ State _____ Zip Code _____ Country _____

☐ For additional information on the National Association of Review Appraisers & Mortgage Underwriters

☐ Check enclosed payable to the NARA/MU

For Credit Card Charges
☐ VISA   ☐ MASTERCARD   ☐ AMER. EXPRESS
Card No. _____ Exp. Date _____
Signature _____ Date _____

INTRODUCTORY OFFER!
"ALL NEW BOOK"
"PRINCIPLES AND TECHNIQUES OF APPRAISAL REVIEW"
$29.50

If You Review Appraisals or if Your Appraisals are Reviewed — This Book Is for You!

Principles and Techniques of Appraisal Review is the only complete authoritative source of review information available. This is the new and revised edition, written by the industry's leading authorities.

This book contains over 430 pages and is written to be a handbook and reference guide to the Professional Reviewer as well as a basic textbook for the occasional Reviewer. If you are reviewing appraisals or having your appraisals reviewed, this new book gives you the data you should know.

PART I: Principles & Techniques
Chapter
1. Prefactory to Appraisal Review
2. Qualifications for a Review Appraiser
3. Duties and Functions of the Review Appraiser
4. Requirement and Methods of the Review Appraiser
5. The Reviewers Final Decision and Recommendations
6. Appraisal Reviewing Administration
7. Common Errors and Deficiencies in Appraisal Reports
8. Appraisal Purpose and the Reviewer

PART II: Review Appraisal Guidelines and Examples
9. Detailed Appraisal Review and Approval
10. Detailed Appraisal Review and Disapproval with Form
11. Consolidated Reviewing Statement — Two Appraisals
12. Appraisal Quality and Variance Report for Individual Property Reviews
13. Spot Check Appraiser Cover Letter and Review Forms
14. Tips on Protecting Your Company from Appraisal and Other Types of Real Estate Risk

Chapter
15. Reviewing Guidelines for the Uniform Residential Appraisal Report
16. Commercial Appraisal Review Checklist

PART III: Appraisal Review
17. Reviewing the Single Family Residence
18. Reviewing a Condominium Appraisal Report
19. Reviewing a Multi-Unit Appraisal for Mortgage Underwriting
20. A Systematic and Uniform Approach to the Commercial Appraisal Review Process
21. Reviewing an Office Building Appraisal Report
22. Reviewing the Shopping Center Appraisal
23. Reviewing Appraisals of Proposed Developments and the Role of Risk Assessment
24. Reviewing Appraisals for Government Agencies
25. Reviewing Appraisals for Relocation Purposes
26. Reviewing for Property Tax Purposes
27. Procedures in Reviewing Easement Appraisals
28. Reviewing Appraisal for Legal Purposes — A Pre-Trial Checklist

---

Order Form
PRINCIPLES & TECHNIQUES OF APPRAISAL REVIEW

Please send me _____ copy(ies) at $29.50 each.   Total $ _____   All orders must be prepaid.

NAME _____ TITLE _____

COMPANY _____

ADDRESS _____

CITY _____ STATE _____ ZIP _____

Make check payable to:

Real Estate Book Publishers
TODD PUBLISHING, INC.
Post Office Box 5837
Scottsdale, Arizona 85261

PLEASE CHARGE TO MY CREDIT CARD:
☐ Mastercard No. _____ Expires _____
☐ VISA No. _____ Expires _____
☐ American Express _____ Expires _____
Signature _____

THE SEAL OF APPROVAL

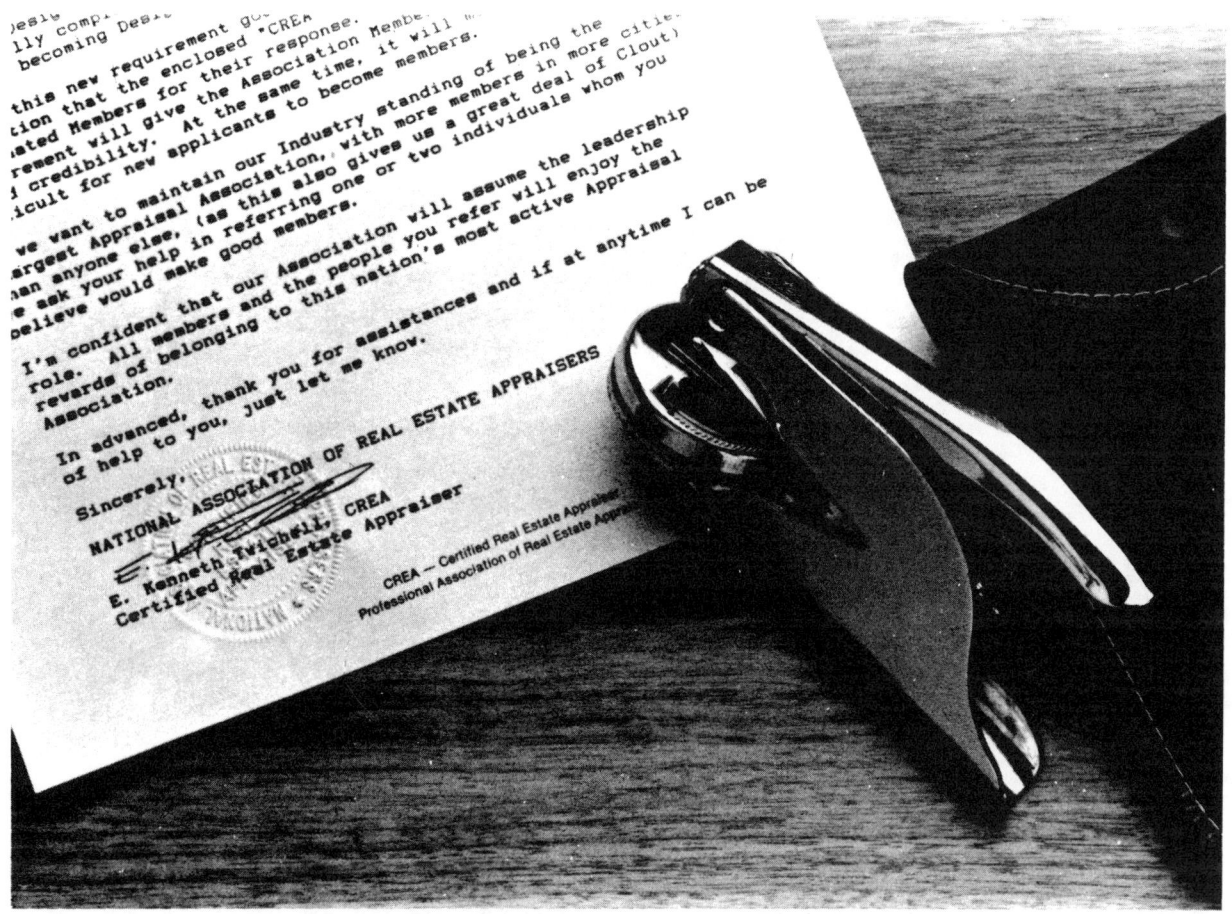

APPRAISAL WITH A RECOGNIZED AUTHORITY

When you are considering the services of a Real Estate Appraiser, consider the advantages of using a member of the nation's largest Appraisal Organization.

"CREA" stands for "Certified Real Estate Appraiser" a designated member of the National Association of Real Estate Appraisers, an organization serving the profession for more than 20 years. To earn the "CREA" designation requires practical appraisal experience, successful completion of a nationally administered examination and adherence to the Association's Code of Professional Ethics.

If you need the services of one of these Professionals, or are contemplating a career in Appraising, contact the National Association of Real Estate Appraisers for further information on the "CREA" designation and its members. Directories are available upon request.

NATIONAL ASSOCIATION OF REAL ESTATE APPRAISERS

8383 East Evans Road
Scottsdale, Arizona 85260-3614
(602) 998-3000

THE INTERNATIONAL REAL ESTATE JOURNAL

If you need to know current and authoritative information on Real Estate happenings **worldwide**, this publication should not be missed.

Receive practical and timely information on Real Estate issues worldwide. The **International Real Estate Journal** will provide you with topics on investments, valuations, development, finance and property management of Real Estate authored by Real Estate professionals from around the world.

Enhance your knowledge and understanding of the International outlooks affecting Real Estate and stay current on International activities that uniquely affect the Real Estate Industry.

Three times a year you will receive in-depth information on Real Estate happenings, trends, and issues on the International market.

ORDER NOW!

THE INTERNATIONAL REAL ESTATE JOURNAL IS AVAILABLE TO YOU FOR THE VERY SPECIAL PRICE OF JUST U.S. $64.00 PER YEAR.

Subscription Form
INTERNATIONAL REAL ESTATE JOURNAL
Please Type or Print Clearly

NAME _____ TITLE _____

BUSINESS AFFILIATION _____

ADDRESS _____

CITY _____ STATE _____ COUNTRY _____ ZIP _____

International Real Estate Institute
8715 Via De Commercio
Scottsdale, Arizona 85258
Telephone: (602) 998-8267
Telex: 165-092

FOR CREDIT CARD CHARGES
☐ Mastercard ☐ Visa ☐ American Express
Charge Amount $ _____
Card Number _____ Expires _____
Signature _____ Date _____
All Orders Must be Prepaid

NOTES

NOTES

NOTES

NOTES